Liturgical Question Box

PETER J. ELLIOTT

Liturgical Question Box

Answers to Common Questions about the Modern Liturgy

IGNATIUS PRESS   SAN FRANCISCO

Nihil Obstat: Reverend G. Diamond, M.A. (Oxon), L.S.S., D. Theol., Diocesan Censor

Imprimatur: Most Reverend Denis J. Hart, D.D., V.G., Auxiliary Bishop

December 22, 1997

Cover by Riz Boncan Marsella

© 1998 Ignatius Press, San Francisco
All rights reserved
ISBN 0–89870–677–7
Library of Congress catalogue number 97–76854
Printed in the United States of America ∞

CONTENTS

Preface 11

Introduction 13

1. The Church and Its Furnishings 21

    1.1 Redesigning the Font and Baptistery 21
    1.2 The Altar and the Celebrant 23
    1.3 The Design of the Altar Today 27
    1.4 Save That Altar! 31
    1.5 The Unlocked Tabernacle 33
    1.6 Veiling the Tabernacle 35
    1.7 Altar Candles 36
    1.8 Ambo Candles? 37

2. Sacred Vessels and Other Objects 39

    2.1 The Book of the Gospels 39
    2.2 Material for Sacred Vessels 40
    2.3 Obliged to Use a Glass Chalice? 41
    2.4 Wine Glasses for the People? 42
    2.5 Blessing a Chalice and Paten 42
    2.6 Blessing Other Vessels 43
    2.7 The Chalice Veil 43

3. Vestments 45

    3.1 Minimum Vestments for Mass 45
    3.2 Chasuble or Stole? 46
    3.3 Stole over the Chasuble? 49

3.4   Stole over a White Habit? 50
3.5   Vestments for Concelebration 50
3.6   Design of Vestments 51
3.7   The Cope at Exposition and Benediction . . 52
3.8   Blessing of Vestments 53

4. Liturgical Ministries 54

4.1   Fed up with Lectors 54
4.2   Sack the Servers? 56
4.3   Behavior of Servers 57
4.4   Female Servers 58
4.5   More Problems 60

5. Ceremonial Actions 62

5.1   Genuflections 62
5.2   When and Where to Genuflect 64
5.3   The Double Genuflection? 65
5.4   Liturgical Dancing? 66
5.5   Incense at Mass 70
5.6   Incense at Exposition and Benediction 70
5.7   Incense without a Server 71
5.8   Bowls of Burning Incense 71

6. During the Liturgy of the Word 73

6.1   Greeting the Assembly Twice 73
6.2   The Alleluia Verse 75
6.3   Using the Book of the Gospels 75
6.4   The Order of the Gospel Procession 77
6.5   Raising the Book of the Gospels? 78
6.6   Lay People Reading the Gospel and
      Preaching 78

6.7   Omitting the Creed 79
6.8   Alternatives to the Creed 80
6.9   General Intercessions on Weekdays 82

7. During the Liturgy of the Eucharist 84

7.1   Preparing the Altar 84
7.2   One Prayer for Offering Bread and Wine . . 85
7.3   Omitting the Washing of the Hands 86
7.4   Congregation Standing during the
        Eucharistic Prayer 87
7.5   Changing the Words of Consecration 89
7.6   Anticipating the Fraction 90
7.7   Genuflecting at the Consecration 93
7.8   One Genuflection after the Elevations? . . . 94
7.9   Deacon Standing at the Consecration 94
7.10 The Memorial Acclamation 95
7.11 Raising the Host at the Doxology 96
7.12 Holding Hands during the Lord's
        Prayer? 97
7.13 Extending Hands during the Lord's
        Prayer 99
7.14 Not Singing the Lord's Prayer? 99
7.15 The Sign of Peace 100
7.16. Moving the Sign of Peace 101
7.17 How to Make the Sign of Peace 102
7.18 Leaving the Altar for the Sign of Peace . . 104
7.19 Deacons or Lay Ministers Breaking the
        Host? 105

8. During and after the Communion Rite 107

8.1   The Celebrant Receiving the Eucharist
        Last? 107

8.2   Simultaneous Communion 108
8.3   Communion in the Hand 109
8.4   Children's Communion 111
8.5   Techniques of Giving Communion 112
8.6   Who Can Distribute the Eucharist? 113
8.7   Genuflecting before Communion 114
8.8   The Communion Plate 114
8.9   Sitting after Communion 115
8.10 Purification of Vessels 117
8.11 Who Can Purify Sacred Vessels? 118
8.12 Purifying the Fingers 119
8.13 The Sacrarium 120
8.14 Reverence for the Blood of Christ 121
8.15 The Blood of Christ in the Sacrarium . . . 122

9. Concelebration 124

9.1   A Concelebrant Reads the Gospel 124
9.2   "At Your Hands"? 125
9.3   Arranging Concelebrants 126
9.4   The Silent Concelebrant 127
9.5   The Doxology at a Concelebrated Mass . . 129
9.6   Communion of Concelebrants 130
9.7   Reaction against Concelebration 130

10. Liturgical and Sacramental Problems 132

10.1 Accidents, Mistakes and Incidents 132
10.2 Unforeseen Problems at Mass 135
10.3 Liturgical Law in Difficult Situations 137
10.4 Desecration of the Holy Eucharist 139
10.5 Confessional Practice after Profanation . . . 140
10.6 Mass Celebrated Alone 144
10.7 Mass Celebrated Alone and Silently? 145

10.8   An Unusual Case of Mass Celebrated
      Alone 145

10.9   Permission for a "Home Mass" 146

11. Sacramental Practice 148

11.1   Reconciliation of Converts 148

11.2   Valid Matter for the Eucharist 150

11.3   Bringing the Eucharist to the Sick 152

11.4   A Pill Box Is Not a Pyx 154

11.5   An Unusual Request 155

11.6   Marriage Facing the People 156

11.7   The Penitential Rite at Nuptial Mass 156

11.8   Blessing Holy Water 157

11.9   The Holy Oils 158

11.10 Cleaning Altar Linen 159

11.11 Disposing of "Old Holy Water" 160

12. Eucharistic Adoration 161

12.1   Regulations for Exposition of the Blessed
      Sacrament 161

12.2   Perpetual Adoration? 162

12.3   Adoration Chapels 164

12.4   Number Present at Benediction 166

12.5   The Minister of Exposition 167

12.6   Interrupting Exposition of the Blessed
      Sacrament 168

12.7   Preaching during Exposition of the Blessed
      Sacrament 170

12.8   The Rosary during Exposition 171

12.9   The Exposition Throne? 172

12.10 Illuminating the Exposition Throne 173

12.11 The Corporal for Exposition 174

12.12 Candles and Lamps during Exposition ... 174

13. Ceremonies during the Church Year 176

13.1 Holy Thursday: Washing of the Feet 176
13.2 Washing Hands instead of Feet? 177
13.3 Good Friday: Veneration of the Cross ... 177
13.4 Rearranging the Easter Vigil 178

14. Funerals 180

14.1 Placing Symbols on the Coffin 180
14.2 Funeral Readings: Poems and Popular
Music? 181
14.3 Homily or Eulogy? 183
14.4 The Color of Funeral Vestments 184

Appendix: The Oxford Declaration on the Liturgy... 187

PREFACE

Most of the questions included in this book were first raised in the "Liturgical Question Box", which has appeared in recent years in *Christ to the World*, an *International Review of Documentation and Apostolic Experiences*. I thank the editors of *Christ to the World*, in particular the Rev. Fr. Alphonse Sutton, F.I., for welcoming the publication of these questions and answers in book form. The questions and replies given in *Christ to the World* have been expanded, adapted and supplemented with new material. Some questions are obviously from clergy and touch on pastoral questions, while others reflect the queries and concerns of the laity. For easy reference, authorities are cited in the text, without abbreviations, and there are no footnotes.

The replies to the questions often reflect and develop various areas I have already covered in *Ceremonies of the Modern Roman Rite* (San Francisco: Ignatius Press, 1995), published in Spanish as *Guia pratica de liturgia* (S.A. Pamplona: Ediciones Universidad de Navarra, 1996). However, this more popular question-and-answer volume provides the opportunity to explain in greater detail and in a more relaxed style themes contained in that manual. Moreover, the scope of this book has been widened to include sacramental questions and various pastoral problems related directly to the celebration of the liturgy and sacraments. *Liturgical Question Box* thus anticipates the sequel that is being prepared to accompany *Ceremonies of the Modern Roman Rite*, that is, a ceremonial guide to the sacraments, funerals and the rites of the Church Year.

I thank the Most Rev. Denis J. Hart, Auxiliary Bishop of the Archdiocese of Melbourne, for his expert advice and incisive comment on technical points. My gratitude is also due to the Rev. Msgr. Alan McCormack, Rev. Kieran Adams, O.P., Rev. Geoffrey H. Jarret, Rev. Peter Joseph, Rev. Michael Miller, C.S.B., Rev. Paul Stuart, Rev. William R. Young and Mrs. Christine McCarthy for their suggestions and advice. They are not necessarily committed to all the opinions offered in this work.

The editorial staff of Ignatius Press have not only shown me cooperation with their many useful suggestions but once again demonstrated that their work is motivated by a deep love for Our Lord Jesus Christ and His beloved Bride the Church.

— Rev. Msgr. Peter J. Elliott

INTRODUCTION

Someone looking in on the Church from the outside must be puzzled, even perplexed, hearing Catholics discuss liturgical questions. A world where men and women, even children, ponder over genuflections, incensations, ambos and acolytes may seem irrelevant to "real life" at the beginning of the third millennium. Of course this is not so, once one realizes that all liturgical matters are part of the color and texture of a most marvellous tapestry, a richer and greater whole. This is the Divine Liturgy itself, that hymn of endless prayer, praise and adoration rising daily from the members of a global community, the People who are united with the Man who is God and the God who became Man, Jesus Christ the Lord.

Therefore, dealing as it must with "all things great and small", this kind of book is meant to be read primarily within the family circle of the Church. So anyone who is not curious about the details of Catholic worship should put *Liturgical Question Box* aside. This book will make as much sense to such a reader as a study of the finer points of bridge would make to someone seeking a treatise on human rights. Of course it would be unjust to imply that people who play bridge cannot be concerned about human rights, but that applies equally to those of us who discuss liturgical questions.

The worship of the Catholic Church is no secret matter. It is a public activity that involves millions of people daily, and, in particular, on every Sunday, in all the nations of the world. Liturgical worship and sacramental life are closely related to the struggle for justice and human rights that today finds its greatest and most consistent champions in the Catholic Church. The right order and balance of Christian worship flow from the Heart of Jesus Christ into our daily lives, because both Christian worship and Christian living are informed by His enduring truths of charity, peace, justice and solidarity.

Liturgical Law?

Catholic worship is meant to be well ordered. Therefore, *Liturgical Question Box* assumes that liturgical law exists and that it is binding. But the purpose of this law is to encourage and promote the spiritual well-being, participation and unity of Christ's faithful. It also exists for the sanctification and protection of the clergy, who celebrate the rites of the Church at the very heart of their ministry to others. It is thus a law of service, not servitude. It is a law that flourishes only within the freedom of grace, because it facilitates the supreme ministry of grace, imparted in the sacraments. Outside the domain of grace, it soon degenerates into formalism and leads to ritualism. But like all sound law, it exists both for the good of the individual person and for the common good of persons. Duly ordered liturgical worship sustains the People of God by maintaining, protecting and promoting the central reason for the existence of the Church, the adoration of the triune God.

Pope John Paul II has explained how liturgical law is concerned with the different roles people play in worship and that liturgical law points beyond itself. On March 8, 1997, speaking to the French bishops of Provence and the Mediterranean, he said:

The liturgy, which expresses the Church's proper nature and is a source for the mission, is given to us by the Church to glorify God: thus *its laws*, which should be respected by distinguishing the *different roles* carried out by the ordained ministers and by lay people. Whatever directs believers to God, what gathers them and what unites them with one another and with all the other assemblies should be given priority. The Council was clear on this matter: "Pastors of souls must, therefore, realize that when the liturgy is celebrated, something more is required than the laws governing valid and lawful celebration. It is their duty also to ensure that the faithful take part fully aware of what they are doing, actively engaged in the rite and enriched by it" (*Sacrosanctum Concilium*, no. 11).

While there are more options and a more flexible pastoral approach is evident today, this is no excuse for a cavalier attitude toward directives, rubrics and traditions. The anarchist approach to liturgy has caused great harm among the Catholic people. It cannot provide that "something more" that the Council Fathers called for, going beyond lawfulness and validity, because it has scorned the foundational structure of Christian worship. Therefore, while I was at first surprised to find so many of the laity taking up *Ceremonies of the Modern Roman Rite* as a guide to "what should be done", their enthusiastic response has taught me a greater sympathy for those faithful families and individuals who worship God in churches where confusion and mistakes still reign.

Responsibility and Competence

In an era when liturgical confusion and innovations linger, Canon 528 §2 places a certain responsibility on parish clergy:

The pastor is to see to it that the Most Holy Eucharist is the center of the parish assembly of the faithful; he is to work to see to it that the Christian faithful are nourished through a devout celebration of the sacraments and especially that they frequently approach the sacrament of the Most Holy Eucharist and the sacrament of penance; he is likewise to endeavor that they are brought to the practice of family prayer as well as to a knowing and active participation in the sacred liturgy, which the pastor must supervise in his parish, under the authority of the diocesan bishop, being vigilant lest any abuses creep in.

Some questions raised here deal more with basic mistakes than with abuses. In my replies to various questions, I have presumed good intentions but without pretending that certain actions are not mistaken, at times destructive and even bizarre. Often these mistakes are due to a lack of good formation in the immediate postconciliar era, when we must admit that there was much uncertainty about liturgical details in the Roman Rite.

Fallen among the Liturgists

At times, this approach leads me to collide with the agenda of *some* liturgists, usually of my own generation. I believe that these men and women are imprisoned in the recent past because they cling to a kind of "Maoist" mythology of a perpetual or "ongoing" liturgical revolution. That mythology is derived from a dated commitment to a permanent program of planned changes rather than to organic and natural development. It has not made these people popular within the wider Church, which they do not always understand. Theologians were the butt of jokes twenty years ago. Now it is the liturgists' turn. I was recently asked: What do you do if you are locked in an elevator with two terrorists and a liturgist, and you have only two bullets in your gun? Reply: Shoot the liturgist—twice.

Humor is often our way of releasing inner tensions and resentments. Not being part of any liturgists' establishment, I feel free to join the Catholic people, not only in the jokes but in their underlying plea to that kind of liturgist—*please leave us alone!* That too is a tension that surfaces in various questions in this book. But a desire to be left alone, to be allowed to pray, should not mean rejecting the active and intelligent participation that is the mind of the postconciliar Church. Rather, it is a plea not to be pushed around any more, whether by some liturgical *führer*, by the mistress of ceremonies or by facilitators of contrived communal joy.

Today a better trend in favor of reverent Catholic worship is evident among younger clergy and religious. They do not carry with them the burden of certain psychological problems related to the recent past. Therefore we may confidently hope that a more settled and constructive era lies ahead when the sacred liturgy will be celebrated carefully and reverently, with a healthy aesthetic sense and with greater respect for the norms of the Church. This can come about when people are aware of the riches that are to hand when sound traditions and norms are recognized for what they are—paths to freedom and spiritual growth.

However, in resolving practical pastoral problems in this field, often a prudent judgment is required in order to discern the preferable course of action or some more convenient and sensible procedure. So, as in *Ceremonies of the Modern Roman Rite*, at various points I offer my own opinions, making it clear in the text where the author's views should be distinguished from a clear-cut interpretation of what the Church requires.

The "Reform of the Reform"

In this work I have also gone farther than I did in *Ceremonies of the Modern Roman Rite* in considering some possible official changes in liturgical practice. I hold a cautious and moderate position with regard to what is called the "reform of the Reform", which can degenerate into a thinly disguised agenda for those who have turned tradition into an ideology. But we dare not hide in the fiction that every detail of the postconciliar liturgical reform was good, or that it was all carried out well, that it was not influenced by the unstable era in which it occurred, or that there is no room for improvement today. Various questions raised in this modest volume imply criticism of what has been authorized since the Council. I respond to some of these criticisms in a rather severe way when they are facile, but there are other critical observations that must be treated with sympathy and honesty. Nevertheless, our first duty is to use, enrich and exploit what we have in the official texts and the resources that have emerged from the liturgical reform. We should also respect the scholarship and dedication of many of those involved in that difficult project. Only then can we begin to make constructive proposals for official improvements.

To this end we surely need to recover the positive spirit that animated the liturgical movement in the decades before the Council. An appeal to return to that spirit, indeed, to reactivate the liturgical movement, is found in the *Oxford Declaration on Liturgy* (1996). This provocative appeal was the fruit of the Liturgy Forum organized by the Centre for Faith and Culture, Westminster College, Oxford. Having participated in the elaboration of this *Declaration*, I am pleased to reproduce it in full as an appendix to this book (p. 187).

Faith and Culture

Liturgy always involves the creative interaction between faith and culture. Readers will note that I have retained references to different cultural contexts and to problems of inculturation. This was necessary in preparing the original replies for publication in *Christ to the World*, which is a pastoral missionary journal read on every continent, especially in those countries that are linked directly to the Congregation for the Evangelization of Peoples. It is important to remember that while our Roman Rite is derived from Europe, this most widespread of the Catholic Rites is meant to be prudently inculturated. That delicate process is not necessarily the path to wild innovation, because true inculturation may also act as a brake on liturgical novelties that may have been imported by priests who have followed "the latest trends" in Europe or North America.

Whatever the cultural context, practical and theoretical liturgical questions will continue to arise. This is a sign of the temporal nature of earthly worship and an indication of its human dimension. Nonetheless, such a human quality shows us how liturgical life is always developing, moving ever forward within our common Christian pilgrimage to the perfect worship that will be heaven. Therefore, I welcome further questions from clergy and laity alike. I hope and pray that in resolving liturgical matters great and small, readers may be helped to offer more worthy worship to the triune God, our loving duty in this life and our beatific reward in the next.

I

THE CHURCH AND
ITS FURNISHINGS

1.1 Redesigning the Font and Baptistery

> All kinds of novel designs for baptismal fonts are appear-
> ing in our diocese. One looks like a bath, another seems
> more like a fountain, and there are water lilies and fish in
> one "baptismal pool", as the pastor calls it. Is this really
> in line with good liturgy and liturgical law?

Just as there was experimentation on the location and form
of the altar some years ago, so the font is now attracting
the attention of liturgists and church architects. In fact, in
the light of this development, we should widen your question to include the whole area where Baptism is celebrated,
the baptistery, which is the focus for the Rite of Christian
Initiation: the Baptism of adults, children or infants.

While there may be novelties, as you suggest, and putting
flora and fauna in the font is absurd, there is a serious need
to rethink the design of the baptistery and the font. The
first consideration should be the *location* of the baptistery.
The common solution of adapting to the new rites of Christian Initiation by merely moving the font into the sanctuary
seems to me to be a clumsy mistake. In effect it destroys the
baptistery, that is, a separate *area* for Baptisms, because the
font is now relegated to a corner of the sanctuary or even

becomes just another object or ornament in the sanctuary. This is not much of an improvement over the small baptistery found in so many of our older churches, a dusty alcove or tiny chapel tucked to one side of the main entrance. That location was not ideal, and indeed it was a modification of the classical Christian tradition that envisaged a separate area, a distinct place, even a separate building for the baptistery, such as we see near some of the great cathedrals in Italy, such as St. John Lateran in Rome and the cathedrals in Florence, Pisa and Parma. That classical tradition is meant to be respected today (cf. *Roman Ritual, Rite of Baptism for Children, Christian Initiation*, general introduction, no. 25). Where, then, can we locate the baptistery in our parish churches today?

In a baptistery ample space is needed for the ceremonies and, above all, a location that symbolically underlines the ecclesial effect of the first of the sacraments, the cleansing from original sin that is a rebirth into the Mystical Body of Christ. Personally, I favor placing the baptistery at or near the main entrance of the church, preferably at the center, so that all have to pass around it. During the celebration of Baptism, those gathered in the nave can turn to it to take part in the Rite, outside or during Mass. This may also be the appropriate place to take holy water on entering the church, an action that recalls our baptism into Christ.

When we concentrate on the heart of the baptistery, the font, the postconciliar rites underline the need to construct a worthy, ample and, indeed, beautiful font. In the words of the *Roman Ritual, Rite of Baptism for Children, Christian Initiation*, general introduction, no. 22, the font is to be "stationary, gracefully constructed out of a suitable material, of splendid beauty and spotless cleanliness". Such a font can be conveniently filled with pure water, even running water and heated water; thus it can easily be cleaned and kept clean. Next to it should be a worthy candlestick, stand or bracket for the Easter candle, which remains here outside the Easter Season. The Holy Oils might well be reserved nearby in a secure and noble repository or in an aumbry, or ambry (wall safe).

Because the first option of baptism by immersion (cf. Canon 854) is being rediscovered, the bowl of the font should be large enough to allow for the immersion of infants. For a simple form of the immersion of adults, a sealed, waterproof area around the base of the font, or a separate section in a two-level font, could be available. Here the adult candidate could kneel in water and have water poured over him or her by the celebrant of Baptism. Taking into account the local culture, and respecting the directives of the episcopal conference (cf. Canon 854), a pool for total immersion could also form the major part of a font, while allowing for the other more widespread option of baptism by effusion (pouring), that is, by including a standing font for this purpose. A good example in this regard is the font in the Cathedral of the Madeleine in Salt Lake City. Bearing in mind that the options for administering Baptism are proposed in one of the earliest Christian documents, the *Didachē*, enthusiasm for immersion must never exclude pouring the water of regeneration. We are not Baptists.

1.2 The Altar and the Celebrant

Some priests were discussing proposals to restore Mass facing the altar. One said that it was forbidden anyway because it was pre-Vatican II. Another said he could not see the point of spending all that money altering the sanctuary in his church if he had to turn his back on the people. What is your opinion?

This question is a good way of introducing a reflection on how we should design altars today and on the purpose and function of the Christian altar. First, let me offer an opinion on which way the priest should face when he celebrates the Liturgy of the Eucharist.

Each passing year one hears of more proposals to restore the celebration of Mass "facing the altar", and, surprisingly, these do not always come from "conservative" liturgical circles. If this proposal were merely "reactionary", that is, based on prejudice or nostalgia, it would be of little value. But there are good spiritual, scholarly, pastoral and aesthetic reasons that favor at least a more open view than the misinformed comments you mentioned.

Personally, I am perfectly at home with either way of celebrating Mass, so I have no "axe to grind" when people argue about this. Moreover, Mass "facing the people" can be very beautiful and inspiring, that is, when the celebrant is recollected and reverent and when he celebrates without haste, with worthy vessels and vestments and at a noble altar. But that is the challenge of Mass "facing the people"; it is more demanding, and it requires greater attention to word, gesture and the visible details, bearing in mind that "everything" is visible. But I believe we should open the door once more to a rich tradition we have almost lost. Therefore I will also present a case for promoting the *option* of celebrating "facing the altar". Ultimately, that case seems to be based on a deeper understanding of the purpose and finality of Christian worship.

We must begin with the facts when discussing this important liturgical question. First, the argument that in the "early Church" Mass was celebrated "facing the people" is no longer pressed by liturgists. The classical tradition was to face East, to welcome the rising light of Christ. In most churches this meant that the celebrant and people faced the same way, and he stood on the same side of the altar as the people, with his back to them. In rare cases, he stood on the other side of the altar facing toward the people. This seems to have been the case when the building itself was not oriented or when there was a grotto for the tomb of a saint in the area immediately in front of the altar, as we see in the basilicas in Rome.

When we come to the recent reform of the Roman Rite, the option of celebrating *ad orientem*, facing East, or "facing the altar", has never been forbidden. Mass "facing the people" was not required by the Council Fathers (who made no reference to it in their Constitution on the Sacred Liturgy, *Sacrosanctum concilium*). It was strongly favored, but never insisted upon, in the postconciliar reforms, but the rubrics of the Roman Missal of Pope Paul VI assume that the priest is not facing the people during the Liturgy of the Eucharist (see the *General Instruction of the Roman Missal*, no. 107, on "Pray brethren . . ." and no. 115 on "This is the Lamb of God"). Nevertheless, the *General Instruction of the Roman Missal*, no. 262, states that the main altar should be freestanding "to allow" Mass "to be celebrated facing the people". The word "allow" does not impose celebrating toward the people. This explains why, in 1993, an editorial essay in Italian appeared in such an authoritative source as *Notitiae* (published by the Congregation for Divine Worship) underlining the value of both options, "facing the people" and "facing the altar" (cf. *Notitiae*, vol. 29, no. 322 [1993]: 245–49).

In 1996, the Eastern Rites received an *Instruction for Apply-*

ing the Liturgical Prescriptions of the Code of Canons of the East-
ern Churches from the Congregation for Oriental Churches.
This *Instruction* also corrects the latest "romanization" that
has infected some Eastern Rites, the urge to "modernize"
by introducing a celebration of the Divine Liturgy "facing the people". In the *Instruction*, continuous tradition and
spiritual interpretations from the Fathers of the Church are
presented, hence: "This rich and fascinating interpretation
also explains the reason for which the celebrant who presides in the liturgical celebration prays facing the east, just
as the people who participate. It is not a question, as is often
claimed, of presiding the celebration with the back turned
to the people, but rather of guiding them in pilgrimage toward the Kingdom, invoked in prayer until the return of
the Lord" (*Instruction*, no. 107). This recently proposed argument might well resonate in the West.

Therefore to characterize facing East as "turning one's
back to the people" misses the point that, when everyone
faces the same way, the priest is leading the people in worship. When he remains on their side of the altar, he is literally "standing with them" in a shared pilgrim journey to
the Kingdom of Christ's dawning light. Moreover, a cumbersome freestanding altar can even set up a barrier between
priest and people, especially when it has the proportions of
a billiard table and seems to push the priest away from the
assembly.

In addition, there is a growing sense of discomfort with
a rite that is usually celebrated so that the only moment
the celebrant does not face the people is during the entrance procession! The transcendent dimension of worship
can be diminished by an unvaried face-to-face encounter
that may last for an hour. The ensuing "horizontalism" is
one cause of much of the dullness that weakens contem-

porary worship. Therefore, while "facing the people" may not be a liturgically correct description, in fact, it accurately describes a practice that spread in the television age and was obviously meant to promote communication, dialogue and instruction. On those pastoral grounds, this style of worship has been an unqualified success for most of the Liturgy of the Word, celebrated at the ambo and chair, but can we say the same for the Liturgy of the Eucharist? It is time at least to be flexible on this issue, because insistence on facing the people is a rejection of an almost universal tradition, which seems to be returning.

1.3 The Design of the Altar Today

> What then is to be done in designing or renovating the altar?

Clearly we should allow space for both options. *New* main altars must be built so as to allow for Mass to be celebrated from *either* side of the altar, that is, so that the altar can be approached on all sides and hence be seen as truly "free-standing". This also rules out building an altar near the edge of a step or placing objects in front of it, thereby preventing priests from celebrating *ad orientem*. That would be just as restrictive as building a new main altar against the wall so as to impede priests from celebrating toward the people.

The *General Instruction* requirement of a truly "freestanding" altar may be interpreted as binding in the case of (a) the main altar of a new church and (b) the altar of a new side chapel regularly used for public worship. However, it is not binding in the case of chapels, side altars or private oratories, and the Pope's private chapel has been cited as a case in point, even if it was constructed at the time of liturgical transition. When chapels or side altars are used mainly for Mass without a congregation, insisting on a freestanding altar would seem to be absurd, since usually there are no people to face!

Some points may be helpful in considering the styles of freestanding altar that are appearing in our churches. There seem to be two unsatisfactory extremes that should be avoided.

1. The first extreme is building an altar that is too large and overpowering. Shortly after the Council, there was a tendency to build long, even cumbersome freestanding altars, perhaps influenced by the ceremonial for concelebration, which may have been misunderstood as requiring every concelebrant to have his own place right at the altar, "just like the Last Supper". Other problems arose in churches where large existing altars were simply brought forward and freed from their gradines (shelves for candles and flowers) and exposition thrones. In some cases, when there was plenty of space, this worked well; in others, the altar did not accord with the lines of vision and the proportions of the sanctuary envisaged by the original architect of the church. More recently other cumbersome altars have appeared, even arranged lengthwise down the church.

2. The opposite extreme has become a more prevalent fashion in recent decades. This is the return to what is supposed to be the primitive table altar. Such a trend has been influenced in English-speaking countries by that largely unreliable puritanical guide *Environment and Art in Christian Worship*, a document whose authority has been grossly exaggerated. With a few exceptions made of fine marble and mosaic, the quest for the primitive table has produced dull altars, certainly not the noble sign that should be the natural

focus of the celebration. Often these tables or plinths are of such reduced proportions, allegedly those of the primitive "cube" shape, that one seems to be looking at a glorified credence table. What may be appropriate in a small oratory is lost in a large sanctuary, and the Christian altar merely becomes another piece of furniture, competing with the ambo, the chair and perhaps the font. Many existing altars that could have been adapted have simply been demolished and replaced by these pathetic mini-altars. A particularly unfortunate example may be seen in the beautiful gothic basilica at the Marian shrine of Pontmain, France.

This reduced form of altar is obviously meant to emphasize the role of the celebrant as he faces the assembly, but this leads to the temptation to turn the altar into a kind of pulpit, as in fact happens at some eucharistic celebrations. A small altar is also often inconvenient, not allowing enough room for extra sacred vessels and the missal or sacramentary. Some of these mini-altars have even been arranged incorrectly, that is, off-center, so that the ambo, chair and altar all have equal value. This may reflect a misguided theology that makes the word equal to the sacrament, and that is not Catholic teaching. The round or triangular altar has even appeared in this context. These are inconvenient shapes for the altar, and by their limited forms (a squat cylinder or angular object) they may even trivialize the most sacred and central sign in the church.

Turning from these extremes, we may consider a more balanced design for a new altar. The first principle is that this eucharistic table is meant to be the great sign of Christ in the church. This building was built to house an altar, which is the rock of sacrifice, the meeting place with God, set aside or dedicated for the Sacrifice of the New Covenant, which is Calvary under a sacramental form. Hence, by its material and proportions the altar should convey a sense of permanence and stability. At the same time it is the holy table of the eucharistic banquet where God's People are nourished by the Body and Blood of the Lord. But it is not a secular table for a domestic meal. The Christian altar is a sacred place for meeting the Lord and entering into sacramental communion with Him and with the members of His living Body, the Church. The whole sanctuary area is the "eucharistic room" where we eat and drink the Body and Blood of Christ, and the altar is the focal point, around and from which, not necessarily at which, Christ's faithful receive the most Holy Gift.

Therefore, the Christian altar should be a majestic, noble object that draws the eye and that does not vanish in its setting. Its proportions should be ample, with due attention to the architect's counsel on lines of vision and the need for enough steps for the people to see the eucharistic action. It can be made of stone or marble, preferably, or of good quality wood, or another durable material approved by the episcopal conference (cf. *General Instruction of the Roman Missal*, no. 263). The material is subject to the final approval of the local Ordinary in the United States. One would hope that glass or plastic would be excluded. A particularly inappropriate glass altar mars the Shrine of Our Lady at Pompeii in Italy. But an altar need not be a monolithic object. A noble stone or marble table resting on columns is ideal for Mass "facing the people", because the priest is no longer presented to the assembly as if he were a talking torso.

If the altar is simple, I suggest that it should be dressed with a noble antependium, of the color of the season or feast. Adorning the altar with a fine cloth and rich hangings goes back to the early Christian centuries, as may be seen in the sixth-century Melchisedech mosaic in the Church of San Vitale in Ravenna, to which I refer elsewhere in this work. The use of an antependium is a good solution when a parish does not have the resources to replace a plain wooden altar with a more permanent one made of stone or marble, or when the altar itself is portable and looks flimsy. It is a way of expressing the sacred in any circumstance, of ensuring that there is a beautiful and worthy table of sacrifice at the heart of even the humblest church or chapel.

1.4 Save That Altar!

Does the existing main altar in every church have to be moved?

This may surprise you, but *no*. As we have seen, there are no grounds for the dogmatism that *all* Masses must be celebrated "facing the people", hence that *all* preconciliar main altars must be rebuilt or demolished. An Ordinary who might want to enforce such a rule should know that the liturgical law of the Church does not permit him to mandate this policy. Again this question has been answered in a balanced way in the aforementioned editorial essay in *Notitiae*, vol. 29, no. 322 (1993): 249, nos. 3–5. This essay adds that where the existing altar is beautiful, of historical value, and *not too distant from the people*, the temporary altar should be removed and the Liturgy of the Eucharist should be celebrated, *ad orientem*, at the existing altar.

When a temporary arrangement has endured for many years, this may indicate not only caution but the providential intervention of local artistic and cultural authorities. Here we should also take account of the question of two competing altars in the same sanctuary, which is obviously a duplication of the great sign of Christ. But this only seems to be a problem when the altars are reasonably close to one another, indicating that the former altar might be relocated and redesigned and that the temporary one should be removed.

When the existing altar is very distant and is worthy of preservation, as is the case in some cathedrals, it may become the place for reserving the Blessed Sacrament. The area in front of it could become the eucharistic chapel. A new permanent main altar may then be built, perhaps on an extension of the sanctuary or in a new sanctuary. The recently completed marble and mosaic sanctuary and altar in St. Patrick's cathedral, Melbourne, Australia, is an example of a magnificent interpretation of the modern liturgical sanctuary, perfectly in keeping with the style and space of one of the world's major Victorian gothic churches.

The reordering of most of our churches should not be regarded as a mistake in itself, because the revised rites do call for some adaptation of the sanctuary. Even in the cases where the original altar remains intact and is used for Mass *ad orientem*, a permanent ambo and suitable presidential chair should always be provided. The *way* the renovation has been carried out raises other questions, but these should be examined according to each case and avoiding generalizations. Some sanctuaries are much improved after a postconciliar renovation; others have been vandalized and ruined, and at great expense. The challenge for the future is to repair the harm done, patiently and carefully, and to build worthy altars that express respect for the options the Church offers us.

1.5 The Unlocked Tabernacle

> Sometimes I celebrate Mass in a seminary chapel where
> the tabernacle has neither lock nor key. The tabernacle is
> in continuous use. Does this contravene any current law?

Yes. Canon 938 §3 states: "The tabernacle in which the
Eucharist is regularly reserved is to be immovable, made of
solid and opaque material, and locked so that the danger of
profanation may be entirely avoided."

Note the clarity of the words of this Canon: "immovable", "solid . . . material", "locked so that . . . danger . . .
may be entirely avoided". Therefore the situation you raise
represents a grave transgression of the law—and a serious
abuse in a surprising situation. This disregard for the law
and its intention in a seminary gives bad example to those
who will soon have responsibility for the custody of the
Blessed Sacrament. In this seminary, perhaps they believe
an atmosphere of study and prayer absolves them from wor-
rying about the profanation of the Eucharist, but (a) this is
a universal liturgical law of the Church, and (b) today seminaries are only slightly more secure than public churches.

I would add that many other tabernacles need to be re-
examined in the light of Canon 938. Security is the first
problem. Some tabernacles seem to be "locked", but they
have the simplest kind of locks, like that in a wardrobe door,
which even a child could force open or pick. Other tabernacles could easily be removed because they are not securely
attached to an altar, wall, ledge, niche or pillar, so as to be
"immovable". Some tabernacles are constructed of the kind
of wood that can easily be broken apart.

While the reference to "opaque material" seems to be
intended primarily to control an *illicit* form of perpetual ex-

position, it also raises the question of security. In a house of women religious and in a country parish church, I have seen tabernacles with a glass door that could easily have been violated. In the modern situation of New Age cults and superstitions, and in countries where there is civil discord, profanation of the Most Holy Eucharist is becoming more widespread, and we have to face this menace in a practical way.

In this regard, the other provisions of Canon 938 show the realistic pastoral intention of the law of the Church.

(a) Canon 938 §4: "For a grave cause, it is licit to reserve the Most Holy Eucharist in another safer and becoming place especially during the night." In practice this refers to reserving the Eucharist in the priest's house, on a temporary or permanent basis, especially in unstable social situations where the tabernacle might be violated. Some Ordinaries extend this provision to allow reservation in the priest's house so that the Eucharist may more easily be taken to the sick and dying, or even for reasons of personal devotion, that is, in the case of a retired priest living far from a church or a frail priest residing in a rectory. The word "becoming" should be noted carefully. A becoming "safer place" would favor a lockable room, set up permanently as an oratory, with a dignified and secure tabernacle and lamp.

(b) Canon 938 §5: "The person who has charge of the church or oratory is to see to it that the key of the tabernacle in which the Most Holy Eucharist is reserved is safeguarded most diligently." This provision places the responsibility for custody of the Eucharist on the pastor or rector of a church or a male or female religious superior, or even a lay person in whose house an oratory has been legally erected. The words "safeguarded most diligently" would require that the key and any duplicate key must be locked away (for example, in a safe) and not merely left in a drawer. Obviously, the key must never be left on an altar or, what is worse, in the door of the tabernacle. In some situations, only certain persons need know where the key is kept. I would add that the key itself should be a distinctive and beautiful object, worthy of the custody of God's most precious Gift.

These practical questions should encourage every pastor to go back to the Code of Canon Law and carefully read the whole of book 4, title 3, chapter 2, "The Reservation and Veneration of the Most Holy Eucharist".

1.6 Veiling the Tabernacle

Is the tabernacle veil obligatory?

It cannot be said to be "obligatory", and attempts in the past to make it so have never quite succeeded. However, the veil is still mentioned as the first sign of the Real Presence, before the sanctuary lamp (*Inaestimabile donum*, no. 85). Nevertheless, the lamp is obligatory according to Canon 940. Veiling the vessel or repository for the blessed Eucharist goes back at least to medieval times, when a silken veil or a canopy of fabric was arranged over the hanging pyx, in which the Eucharist was habitually reserved above the altar. A few of these veils have survived in museums, and their fine workmanship shows a particular labor of love and devotion on the part of the unknown souls who made them.

Common sense and good taste should guide us here. If the tabernacle is not an object of artistic value in itself, or especially if it is rather ugly, then the veil should be used. This is especially relevant in the case of a freestanding domed tabernacle, which seems intended to be veiled. But when this kind of tabernacle is covered with the ample veil, or *conopaeum*, it becomes a sacred place, harking back to a biblical sign of the Lord Emmanuel making his "tabernacle" among us in the holy tent. This veiling also enhances a sense of mystery at the place of reservation, conducive to prayer.

On the other hand, if the tabernacle is a fine work of art, richly adorned with enamels, jewels or repoussé work, then it would seem somewhat illogical to conceal it with a veil. In this regard, there are some variations of the veil that allow a work of art to be presented while the sign of the veil remains. In the Holy Father's private chapel in the Apostolic Palace, built by Pope Paul VI, the veil covers only the roof and the sides of the tabernacle and does not hide the finely worked silver and enamel doors.

One feature of the beautiful classical or gothic altars promoted by the preconciliar liturgical movement was the matching antependium and tabernacle veil. Even in our era, when the tabernacle may be located elsewhere, the use of antependia for the altar and ambo and a matching veil for the tabernacle has much to commend it, not only in aesthetic terms but as a way of emphasizing the color of the season or day. The liturgical colors here create a distinctive environment for the eucharistic celebration that visibly relates the action of worship on this day to sacred time and the Church Year.

1.7 *Altar Candles*

> Is there really a "correct" number of candles to use on the altar at Mass?

There are only four possibilities in the Roman Rite: two, four, six and seven candles (cf. *General Instruction of the Roman*

Missal, no. 79). The last possibility applies only when the Ordinary celebrates a Mass, according to a solemn form. The use of one or three candles on the altar is not envisaged in the modern rite and seems to have arisen when flowers replace candles on one side of the altar. However, a good custom has arisen of using two candles for ferial days and memorials, four candles for feasts, and six for Sundays and solemnities (at least at more solemn sung celebrations). Standardizing the number of candles was an element in the Tridentine liturgical reform, aimed at correcting abuses that linked a "mystical" number of candles to certain votive Masses.

The candles are to be placed on or near the altar. "Near" refers to candles in standard candlesticks, but it should imply a visual link with the altar, for these altar candles are not to be confused with the extra candles and lamps that may also adorn the sanctuary on festive occasions, such as the Epiphany. There is no rule as to how they are to be arranged, but I would counsel against the domestic fashion of putting two candles at one end of the altar and a bowl of flowers at the other. Dignified symmetry seems best for the Mass, and placing flowers directly on an altar, especially when it is freestanding, is not part of the classical Roman tradition.

1.8 Ambo Candles?

In some churches, candles stand on each side of the ambo or lectern. These are lit during the Liturgy of the Word and then extinguished. Two candles are then lit at the altar. Is this correct?

I have seen this practice, but there is no authority for it at all, neither in tradition nor in the *General Instruction of the Roman Missal.* It overemphasizes the distinction between the Liturgy of the Word and the Liturgy of the Eucharist, to the point of symbolically separating the two phases of the one liturgy. Moreover, candles at the ambo are only brought there by servers at the reading of the Gospel, to honor Christ in His Holy Gospel, an ancient custom common to the liturgies of East and West. They are not brought there for the other readings from the New or Old Testament, because these come to their fulfillment only in Christ "our Light". Furthermore, having unlit candles on or at the altar during Mass or any other public celebration is not envisaged in the modern rites and seems rather boring. The altar lights mark the time of a whole celebration of word and sacrament.

2

SACRED VESSELS
AND OTHER OBJECTS

2.1 The Book of the Gospels

> I notice that a rather elaborate Book of the Gospels is
> now used in some parishes during Mass. I know this book
> is used at a Solemn Mass, for example in cathedrals and
> abbeys, but I have not been accustomed to using it in a
> parish. Should it be used?

Yes. The revival of the wider use of the Book of the Gospels
is an important feature of the renewal of the Roman Rite. Before the development of Low Mass, the Book of the Gospels
was a central object in all eucharistic celebrations, as it still
is in the Eastern Rites. This sacred object, in fact, ranks first
after the eucharistic vessels. Therefore the use of this book
is not a question of places, such as cathedrals, abbeys, parish
churches or chapels of religious houses. *Every church* should
own such a book because its use is once more a normal part
of our Roman Rite, and the Book is not even reserved for
use at a Solemn Mass.

The Book of the Gospels should be handsomely bound
in the finest leather or covered in fine fabric or embroidery,
perhaps of the color of the day or season. Preferably, according to a noble tradition common to the East and the
West, it should be kept within richly worked covers of pre-

cious metal or elaborately carved wood, and even adorned, if the means allow, with enamels, jewels, gems, ikons, and so on. The main ikon or base relief could appropriately be of Christ our Lord as "Pantokrator", or Christ the Incarnate Word in the arms of the Blessed Mother. Outside liturgical celebrations, this sacred book is kept in the sacristy, not left out in the church, even on or near the ambo. If it is an object of value, it is best kept locked in the safe with the sacred vessels.

2.2 *Material for Sacred Vessels*

> Pottery and glass chalices are on sale in some religious shops. Are chalices made of glass, crystal or ceramics permissible?

Chalices made of glass and ceramics in fact are not envisaged in the Roman Rite. Concerning the materials used for sacred vessels, the *General Instruction of the Roman Missal*, no. 290 says "preference is to be given to materials that do not break easily or become unsuitable". The cup of a chalice is to be made of "nonabsorbent material" (*General Instruction of the Roman Missal*, no. 291).

The question of what constitutes an "easily breakable" chalice is resolved by two practical questions: (a) What happens when this chalice falls on the ground? (b) What happens when the server or celebrant knocks the cruet against the lip of this chalice? The answers to these questions, which embody common incidents, are obvious to anyone who has seen cracked, patched and chipped ceramic chalices, which have also clearly *become unsuitable* due to use since the time they came into vogue in the 1970s. The fact that some religious supply companies continue to sell such vessels does not mean they are licit or suitable for the liturgy.

A chalice made of durable precious stone, for instance, could be unbreakable, and some of these may be seen in museums. A chalice consisting of a metal cup set firmly into a secure base or surround of noble glass, enamel or ceramics is permissible according to the *General Instruction*, no. 291. But worthiness is a further dimension of this problem. Rarely does one see chalices made of glass or ceramics that are worthy of the Eucharistic Sacrifice. Certainly vessels made of fine crystal may be worthy and are often of value, but they are also very fragile, as those who use them discover.

2.3 Obliged to Use a Glass Chalice?

> From time to time I supply in a parish where a glass goblet is put out for me to use, together with a ceramic paten. I feel uncomfortable about this. Am I obliged to use these vessels?

No priest can be obliged to do anything contrary to the official provisions of the Roman Rite. In the situation you mentioned, you should politely ask for a metal chalice, which would surely be available. If it is not available, feel free to bring one to the church yourself—and gently and prudently remind the pastor about respecting other priests' consciences!

As for the ceramic paten, this might be tolerated, provided it is a worthy vessel. The *General Instruction*, no. 292, allows greater freedom for the material chosen for patens, monstrances, cruets, and so on. Behind this flexibility is the question of inculturation, because reference is made to "materials that are prized in the region, for example, ebony or other hard woods, as long as they are suited to local use". Therefore the *General Instruction*, no. 290, speaks of "materials that are solid and in the particular region are regarded as noble". But the local episcopal conference has the final say in determining these matters.

2.4 Wine Glasses for the People?

In one parish I know, the people drink the Precious Blood from wine glasses. Surely this is not allowed.

In parishes where the people drink from the chalice, an appropriate set of smaller metal chalices might well be used, but never wine glasses. As already noted, not only are such vessels excluded by the principle of durability, but there is a clear rule that secular vessels are not to be used at Mass. The instruction from the Congregation for Divine Worship, *Inaestimabile donum*, no. 16, rules out "simple baskets and other vessels for ordinary use outside the sacred celebration". Because an ecclesiastical shop sells a wine glass or glass goblet does not magically turn it into a chalice! Moreover, as anyone who washes dishes knows it is also more difficult to clean drinking vessels made of glass or ceramics, which adds a further complication to the purifications.

2.5 Blessing a Chalice and Paten

Can any priest bless a chalice and paten now?

Yes. But (a) he must first determine that these vessels are made in accord with the law of the Church, indicated in the reply to the previous question, and (b) he must use the special rite for the *Blessing of a Chalice and Paten* provided in the *Roman Pontifical*. This rite may be celebrated either during Mass, just before the preparation of the gifts, or outside of Mass. The chalice is no longer anointed with Chrism during this rite. In fact, if one studies the rite carefully, the first use of the vessels at Mass really sets them apart for sacred service.

2.6 Blessing Other Vessels

Must the ciborium (used at Mass and for reserving the Eucharist) and the small pyx (for the Communion of the sick) be blessed before use?

Yes. Any priest may bless these new eucharistic vessels, provided they are in accord with the law of the Church, cf. *General Instruction of the Roman Missal*, nos. 290–92 and 294. The appropriate prayers are providing in the *Book of Blessings*.

2.7 The Chalice Veil

I notice that the chalice veil is being used in some churches, for example at the side altars of St. Peter's Basilica in Rome. Should the veil be used?

Yes. In fact the chalice veil is now obligatory. The *Ceremonial of Bishops*, no. 125, clarifies the *General Instruction of the Roman Missal*, no. 80 c. The veil is to be of the same color as the vestments of the Mass, but it may always be white, for example, if colored veils are not available. It seems preferable for the veil to be made of the same fabric as the vestments. The use of the burse, a matching square wallet for the corporal, is not mentioned in modern documents, but this is still used in some places because it keeps the folded corporal in good condition.

Except at a Mass celebrated without a congregation, the veiled chalice is set on the credence table, not the altar. Servers must be trained on how to unveil and veil the chalice, because a server brings the chalice to the altar at the beginning of the preparation of the gifts. It is either unveiled on the altar or before it is brought to the altar. During the Liturgy of the Eucharist, its seems preferable to leave the veil folded on the credence table. After the purifications, which are best carried out at the credence table, the chalice is veiled again.

The veil shows traditional respect for the sacred vessels. Moreover veiling and unveiling the chalice helps delineate the different stages of the eucharistic celebration, that is, the transition from the Liturgy of the Word to the Liturgy of the Eucharist. While the kind of veil we see today may be regarded as a late medieval development, and was unknown in some of the pre-Reformation rites and uses, for example in England, it was required from the sixteenth century on, which makes it a well-established custom. Those ordering or making eucharistic vestments should henceforth ensure that a matching chalice veil is part of the whole set.

3

VESTMENTS

3.1 Minimum Vestments for Mass

What vestments should be worn by the priest at Mass?

The minimum vestments are "the chasuble, worn over the alb and stole" (*General Instruction of the Roman Missal*, no. 299, see also nos. 81 a and 161 and the *Ceremonial of Bishops*, no. 66). The priest may also wear an amice under his alb and a cincture to gather the alb and perhaps to secure the stole. As noted elsewhere, the stole is worn under the chasuble. These are the obligatory vestments envisaged in Canon 929, which refers back to the "rubrics" of the *General Instruction*.

There are a few limited exceptions. Concelebrants are not obliged to wear the chasuble, but at a concelebrated Mass the principal celebrant must always wear it. When concelebration is a regular part of liturgical life, such as in religious communities, seminaries and houses where a number of priests reside, surely chasubles should be available for all who concelebrate, at least a matching set in white but preferably in all the liturgical colors. The principal celebrant's chasuble may have a distinctive design or some extra ornamentation to indicate his presidential role. In some countries an indult was given for the celebrant to wear a combined chasuble-alb, but only when celebrating

Mass outside a sacred place. Concelebrants may also wear this garment, which I criticize below.

3.2 Chasuble or Stole?

> I hear that some priests celebrate Mass without a stole, since the chasuble would often cover it. Is this omission lawful? On the other hand, some priests celebrate Mass wearing only an alb and stole. Is that lawful?

The first practice you raise is not lawful, and it seems point-less. I have only encountered it in France. Canon 929 says that "In celebrating and administering the Eucharist, priests and deacons are to wear the liturgical vestments prescribed by the rubrics." As already noted above, the rubrics are found in the *General Instruction of the Roman Missal*, nos. 298–300, 302, and for concelebration, no. 161. Therefore, if a stole is available, the celebrant should wear it, even if it does not match the color of his chasuble, as may happen in a difficult situation.

However, the more widespread and serious rejection of Canon 929 occurs when the celebrant, or principal cele-brant, puts aside the chasuble and wears only an alb and stole. Wearing the alb and stole when celebrating Mass has been permitted in some regions, but only when Mass is celebrated *outside a church or oratory*. In these circumstances, for convenience, a combination alb-chasuble is also allowed, and this may also be worn by concelebrants. It is a rather ungainly garment, and I would never recommend it. I hope that this local permission will be withdrawn because it is contrary to a common tradition in the East and the West. Moreover, it has been a source of minimalism and bad taste because some clergy have chosen to regard it as a universal indult, and it has led in turn to the habit of abandoning *the* eucharistic vestment altogether.

Some might argue that it is more convenient in mission situations to set aside the chasuble, especially when it is hot and a priest must travel far to offer Mass. But a worthy lightweight chasuble can always be taken to the most distant village or mission station. That kind of gesture tells the people that their "humble" Mass is just the same as a grand celebration in the cathedral. Wherever we offer the Lord's Sacrifice, let us always avoid minimalism at His altar and choose dignity, majesty and beauty!

One also wonders *why* the chasuble is set aside, because this decision may not always be only a bad habit or minimalism. Studying the customs of worship among other Christians might show us what is at stake in terms of basic symbols.

At the Reformation, the more extreme Protestants rejected the chasuble because they understood its sacrificial meaning. It was the priestly garment of the Mass as distinct from the pastor's gown or vicar's surplice worn at a memorial Lord's Supper. The more conservative Lutherans never rejected the chasuble, especially in parts of Scandinavia, and one notes that their eucharistic theology was more Catholic in tendency than that of Calvinists and Zwinglians. Later, in the mid-nineteenth century, some Anglicans began to reintroduce the chasuble. Some of these high-church clergymen even went to prison for wearing it. They knew what it means, even if a few of our priests today seem to have forgotten. The chasuble is *the* eucharistic vestment par excellence, reserved for those ordained into the sacrificing priesthood of Jesus Christ. It signifies the charity with which He clothes our weakness at the altar, when indeed we do act *in persona Christi*.

Let me add some remarks on current trends and a related question. The habit of wearing only an alb and stole for Mass became dominant in France in the decades after the Council, but in recent years the good example of younger priests is promoting a return to liturgical normality. This is also evident in the recovery of the priest's distinctive street dress. Religious sociology offers an interesting insight. Clergy who disguise themselves as laity become invisible pastors; this is a characteristic of élite sects, where all the members know the leader personally, by his face. One finds it among the Pentecostalists. It is also a necessary characteristic of a Church under total persecution, as was the situation in Mexico. But it is not characteristic of the Universal Church, enjoying religious freedom to worship and evangelize.

When priests present themselves as visible signs of the Lord Jesus and His true Church, they become signs in the secular society of Christ's mission of service, and they indicate their availability to all people, not only to members of the Church. That too is part of Catholic sacramentality—and "catholicity". In 1979, in his first Holy Thursday letter to priests, Pope John Paul II underlined the need to bring God back to the streets in this way. We may see this today in terms of pre-evangelization. When nonbelievers or fallenaway Catholics see an identifiable priest or religious, they immediately think of God, even if only in some vague way. They are confronted with a whole dimension of life and human experience that otherwise would remain hidden. The city set on a hill is not meant to be concealed, and what we say for Christ is meant to be proclaimed from the rooftops.

3.3 Stole over the Chasuble?

It may seem a small point, but is it right to wear the stole over the chasuble?

The novel fashion of wearing the stole over the chasuble began in Central Europe not long after the Second Vatican Council. Several vestment houses specialized in designing stoles and chasubles along these lines. Although this fashion is steadily fading, the point needs to be made that there are clear instructions that the celebrant is to wear the stole *under* his chasuble (cf. *General Instruction of the Roman Missal*, no. 299, *Ceremonial of Bishops*, nos. 66, 126).

From a symbolic point of view, wearing the stole over the chasuble overemphasizes the stole and reduces the chasuble to a mere background vestment or a setting for an ornamental stole. This may explain why the chasuble was soon discarded in favor of an ample kind of alb, especially in the countries where this fashion prevailed. But here we have an interesting paradox. The stole symbolizes authority in sacramental ministry and preaching. As already noted, the chasuble signifies charity, the love of God that "covers all things" (Colossians 3:14). What should predominate in celebrating the Eucharist—divine love or ecclesial authority?

From an aesthetic point of view, unless designed by experts who know how to avoid exaggerated proportions, the stole arranged over the chasuble does not look good. The "bulky" effect is particularly noticeable when such vestments are worn by shorter celebrants! Thus the chasuble was often discarded in favor of a tailored alb, because this is better suited to "set off" the stole. But then we have the same vestments, stole and alb, for celebrating all seven sacraments and no distinctive vestment for the eucharistic liturgy, the "summit and source" of sacramental life. The wisdom of the continuity of our tradition once more stands vindicated.

3.4 Stole over a White Habit?

> Recently, at a concelebration, I noticed a priest wearing a stole over his white religious habit. He told me that this was permitted in his Order.

Priests who wear white habits or white cassocks cannot substitute these robes for the alb when celebrating or concelebrating Mass. They either put an alb on over their habit or, if the climate is hot, they may remove the habit and replace it with an alb. As far as I can ascertain, no privilege has ever been given in this regard to any Order or Congregation, but legends have always been invoked to justify liturgical laziness and minimalism.

3.5 Vestments for Concelebration

> What vestments are to be worn at a concelebrated Mass?

The chief celebrant must always wear the alb, stole and chasuble, of the color of the day, at a concelebrated Mass. Concelebrants wear the same vestments, in white if a set in the appropriate color is not available. They may wear only an alb and stole, "for a good reason . . . as when there are more concelebrants than vestments", *General Instruction*, no. 161. This concession implies that those in charge of churches or oratories where concelebration is normal should see to it that enough chasubles are available for all who concelebrate. For aesthetic reasons, these vestments should be of good quality and harmonious in color and design. The vestments of the principal celebrant should be distinctive, so that his presiding role is expressed clearly.

3.6 Design of Vestments

> I have noticed some sets of vestments on which no cross or Christian symbol appears, often on the stole and even at times on the chasuble. What are the regulations, if any, about this?

There are no binding regulations. However, taking the *continuity of our tradition* as a guide, there is much to be said for having a cross embroidered on the back of a stole and of maintaining the gracious custom of kissing it before assuming this vestment.

Chasubles now take various forms. In times past some form of the cross or a Christian symbol was virtually universal on this distinctive eucharistic vestment. There was even a beautiful spiritual symbolism in this—the cross on the chasuble encompassed the whole body of the priest when he assumed the vestment before going to the altar to offer the Holy Sacrifice. Therefore, I would counsel respect for that tradition but at the same time would avoid the fussy tendency to embellish vestments with too many signs and symbols. The "material and form", the fine fabric and gracious shape of the vestment, are more important than decorations on it (cf. *General Instruction of the Roman Missal*, no. 306). The chasuble may also be regarded as a whole spiritually. As already noted, it represents putting on the charity of Christ that "covers all things" (Colossians 3:14).

The ornamentation on some stoles and chasubles has "moved" in recent years. Rather than a concentration of symbolic embroidery or appliqué on the back of a chasuble, it is now common to find a sacred symbol worked on the front, so it can be seen during the celebration of Mass "facing the people". The decoration on the stoles worn for celebrating the sacraments is now often found at the level of the priest's chest rather than at each end of the stole.

We also find a timely warning in the *General Instruction of the Roman Missal*, no. 306: "Representations on vestments should consist only of symbols, images, or pictures portraying the sacred. Anything out of keeping with the sacred is to be avoided." But who decides what is out of keeping? Priests will use their common sense, but homemade vestments, presented with the best of intentions, can be embarrassing. In cases that cause scandal, the local Ordinary should intervene, for example if trivia were to appear on vestments (smiling faces and animals adorning a "special vestment" for children's liturgy) or if political symbols were to preach at us from a stole.

On the other hand, appropriate inculturation should influence the form, design and fabric of vestments (cf. *General Instruction of the Roman Missal*, nos. 304–5). In Africa this has generally been done well. In parts of Latin America some multi-colored garments seem neither liturgical nor culturally appropriate. Nevertheless, in all these situations, the episcopal conference raises the possibilities with the Holy See, which has to approve proposals before changes or adaptations can proceed at the local level.

3.7 *The Cope at Exposition and Benediction*

Does the celebrant have to wear a cope at the beginning of exposition? Is the cope obligatory during the rite of Benediction?

The celebrant, a priest or deacon, *may* wear a cope to *begin* exposition in either the simple or solemn form. If the exposition is prolonged, for instance, at a silent Holy Hour or a day of adoration, it would suffice to wear an alb or cassock and surplice and a white stole when exposing the Blessed Sacrament. However, the celebrant *must* wear a cope for the rite of Benediction with the monstrance. He *may* also wear a cope for simple Benediction with the ciborium, although an alb or cassock and surplice and a stole suffice and would seem preferable. But the humeral veil is always worn for the eucharistic blessing, both for the simple and the solemn rite.

If exposition with the monstrance is only for a short time, for instance, for one celebration of prayers, litanies, readings, and so forth, concluding with Benediction, the celebrant incenses the Blessed Sacrament both during the first hymn of adoration and during the hymn for Benediction. He wears the cope for the whole rite. This obviously also applies if the Liturgy of the Hours is sung or recited in the context of solemn adoration.

3.8 Blessing of Vestments

Which, if any, of the vestments and linen used in the Mass must now be blessed beforehand?

The eucharistic vestments, the chasuble, dalmatic, stole and alb, are to be blessed before use. Any priest may bless these vestments using the prayer provided in the *Book of Blessings*. A new corporal and a new altar cloth must be blessed before use, and new purifiers (purificators) and chalice palls should also be blessed. It is fitting to bless a new cope, humeral veil and choir dress, also using the prayer provided in the *Book of Blessings*.

4

LITURGICAL MINISTRIES

4.1 Fed up with Lectors

> I am sorry, but I am sick of listening to boring or un-
> intelligible readers at Mass. Why don't the priests do all
> the readings, as they used to?

There is no need to apologize! I can assure you that priests
are also irritated by incompetent lectors, to use the correct
term for those authorized to read at Mass. But if we priests
grumble, we should realize that we are often responsible for
allowing untrained people to read at Mass.

Every lector must be trained to read in public, and that
is an art in itself. The parish liturgical committee should
concentrate on this task. In fact, the United States is well
ahead in this area of liturgy training, and one encounters
fewer regrettable examples of reading at Mass in the U.S.
than in some other countries.

But you asked why the priest cannot do all the readings,
as was the case up to the mid-sixties. This question leads us
to consider the reasons for the wider renewal of Catholic
worship in its dimension of liturgical ministries and roles.

The variety of liturgical ministries open to laity is strongly
underlined in the major documents of the liturgical reform
and renewal that followed the Council. This development
was not intended by the Council primarily "to involve the

laity". It was to show forth the hierarchical structure of worship more clearly, that is, God's People using the consecration each has received in Baptism, Confirmation and, in some cases, Holy Orders. One of the greatest theologians of the last century, Matthias Scheeben, "the German Newman", taught that the indelible character we receive in these sacraments literally creates the structure of the Church. But that structure is ordered for divine worship. We are baptized, confirmed or ordained first and foremost to be empowered for worship, for the Divine Liturgy. The roles we play in worship express the meaning of the sacraments we have received.

Before the Second Vatican Council, this hierarchy of liturgical ministries was evident only at the gracious celebration of Solemn High Mass. The celebrant was assisted by a deacon, who chanted the Gospel, a subdeacon, who chanted the Epistle, by acolytes, thurifer, and others, and a choir sang the proper, verses from the psalms, and so forth. What we have now is the opportunity to extend that tradition of a hierarchy of liturgical ministries to all other public celebrations of Mass. The lector at Mass today in fact has replaced the subdeacon of the High Mass, not the priest. Introducing lectors can thus be seen as a return to a good tradition that had never been completely lost.

We were also told, correctly, that Solemn Mass was the norm for all forms of Mass, but in practice most parishes rarely, if ever, saw the splendid ceremonies of the Solemn Mass. Before the Council, the Low Mass was the normal form of liturgy in most parish Masses on Sundays and weekdays, and the priest read the Gospel and the Epistle. In some countries, a layman would read a translation at the same time, which was a hint of what would come with the Second Vatican Council's Constitution on the Sacred Liturgy,

Sacrosanctum concilium, nos. 28 and 29, which also called for those carrying out the variety of ministries to be imbued with the spirit of the liturgy. The Council made possible the ministry of lector especially by introducing the celebration of Mass in the vernacular.

The use of the vernacular, Mass celebrated in the language of the people, is surely one of the greatest pastoral gains since the Council—and I say that as a man who loves Latin and believes it should still enjoy an honored place in our worship. The vernacular readings of the lectionary are a great treasury, to nourish and guide us, but they are meant to be read clearly, intelligently and with some style. So I return to the basic requirement of training our lectors well.

4.2 Sack the Servers?

Is there anything in current directives that recommends having a Mass server whenever possible? Some priests have even discouraged boys from serving, saying "Serving is not at all necessary today." In some places it is difficult to find a server now.

The *General Instruction of the Roman Missal*, no. 68, assumes that there will be "other ministers", servers or a server, at public Mass. The role of the server is a normal part of the variety of "special ministries", so strongly emphasized in the post-Vatican II reform. Priests who discourage serving simply do not understand the modern liturgy, nor do they appreciate the value of involving boys and young men in a liturgical ministry that so often encourages vocations to the sacred priesthood. While there is no *obligation* to have a server at Mass, the "self-service" celebrant represents a sorry misunderstanding of the richness of our liturgy, and

the variety of ministries that should be evident in our sanctuaries. But he may also imagine that "Servers don't do much
in the liturgy these days anyway."

Once we rid our minds of the old concept of servers
mainly "answering the Mass" and study what the server *can*
do, we discover that in fact servers have more duties in the
modern rite. For example: a server holds the missal before
the celebrant at the chair; servers may carry cross and candles even at a said Mass; a server should prepare the altar, which involves unfolding the corporal and setting up
the vessels and then removing the vessels and corporal after
Communion. In fact, duties once restricted to the subdeacon (and now granted to adult acolytes) may be carried out
by a *well-trained* boy of ten! So much for the opinion that
serving is not necessary or is a minimal role today.

4.3 *Behavior of Servers*

> I have heard that one of the modern Popes asked that
> there be only one server at Low Mass, I think to prevent
> little boys from talking to one another or being frivolous.
> Is there any ruling on this matter?

No, but one or two servers certainly suffices for a said weekday Mass, which would approximate the old "Low Mass".
However on Sundays, it is good to involve several servers
ministering at the altar, because even at a said Mass, a cross
bearer, book bearer and two candle bearers ("acolytes") can
assist. All Sunday celebrations should be marked by some
exterior solemnity and a variety of liturgical ministries.

I cannot trace the papal request you mention. But the
practice of four or six small boys marching out into the
sanctuary to serve a Low Mass was always poor liturgy. Un-

fortunately, this practice lingers in some parishes. Three further points need to be made in this regard.

1. We have all seen younger servers misbehave, even to the point of disrupting the celebration of the liturgy. But *small children should not be serving Mass*. A minimum age should be set, about ten (in most countries, level five of primary education), and these older children should be trained carefully and put "on probation" until they have proved themselves. We need to get away from the sentimental idea of the "little altar boy" and recover the privilege, dignity and adult status of ministry at the altar, for which older children are the junior apprentices.

2. To put many children at the altar just for show or simply "to involve them" is pointless—because they have no duties to perform. Idle and bored children soon start to chatter and misbehave. However, noting what I have said above, a *reasonable* number of servers can assist at any Mass, carrying out the duties of the cross, the book and processional candles.

3. If servers are misbehaving, this may mean that they have not been trained properly in how to serve, with discipline and order. Unfortunately, it may mean that they lack adequate catechesis on the meaning of the Mass, the Holy Sacrifice and the Real Presence, and the reverent behavior before Our Lord that flows from eucharistic doctrine. Systematic catechesis of servers is essential as well as some discrete supervision of their sacramental and spiritual life.

4.4 *Female Servers*

I know that now the bishop can permit female servers in his diocese. Can he require me to have "altar girls"?

What am I to do if I am appointed to a place where there are "altar girls"?

First, let us never use the trivial terms "altar girls" or "altar boys". The term "servers" is the correct description of the ministries set out in the *General Instruction of the Roman Missal*, no. 68. But, taking up the main theme of your question, while it is clear that the bishop can permit female altar servers, he cannot oblige any priest to have female servers in his parish. One would hope that the bishop would not want to give such an authoritarian impression to his clergy on an optional matter, which is, moreover, only a liturgical concession. Male servers remain the universal norm.

On the other hand, when deciding whether to permit female servers in his diocese, the bishop himself is not bound by another bishop's decisions, even the consensus of the episcopal conference. In some countries, in dialogue with other members of the episcopal conference, he will have to make a prudent decision on this matter, guided by a discerning sense of inculturation. In certain traditional cultures it may not be regarded as appropriate for females of any age to carry out ritual activities in the sanctuary. In other cultures it may be more acceptable.

Your question also indicates that you are not happy about this development. However, rash actions, easily interpreted as intolerance, can cause pastoral harm in any situation. Were you to arrive in a new parish and summarily dismiss the female servers, the effect on these young ladies and their families could cause damage to the community and impair your own priestly ministry. The same prudence and sensitivity apply were you to visit another parish and find girls or young women waiting to serve your Mass. Respect for the pastor of that parish, if he is acting within diocesan law, would also need to be taken into account. If this matter is a personal burden, and you regularly "supply" in that parish, you could request that only males be rostered to serve your Mass.

4.5 *More Problems*

But hasn't the arrival of female servers created problems?

The arrival of female servers raises some practical pastoral questions that could lead to problems. We need to reflect honestly and carefully on some aspects of this development and work out balanced ways of resolving any problems, real or foreseen.

Parents tell us that boys, before and even during puberty, are not always comfortable when sharing public duties with girls. This accounts for the regrettable absence of male servers in some parishes, where it seems as if "the girls have taken over" in the sanctuary. But the prudent pastor can resolve this problem with some careful planning and reorganization—or by retaining the ancient tradition of male servers, as is his right.

Preparing a servers' roster with *separate teams for boys and girls* is one sensible and just response to the natural reluctance of boys to serve with girls. Teams of teenage or adult servers may be mixed, but prudence is required here, bearing in mind that this may not be appropriate in traditional cultures. In less traditional cultures the pastor should see that these mixed teams of young people are carefully supervised.

Because the Church teaches that sex, or "gender", is an objective reality, some distinctive dress for female servers may seem advisable. While the alb may seem visually appropriate for a female server, in my opinion, the cassock and surplice should never be worn by a girl or a woman. The cassock and surplice is *choir dress for male clerics*, extended by custom to young male servers, and this custom is rejected by various liturgists since boys are not clerics. But choir dress conjures up a male "clerical image", so a female wearing male robes could be described as a bizarre ecclesiastical form of "cross-dressing". Wearing robes with a visible masculine ecclesiastical association can only serve the interests of a few dissenters who still favor the ordination of women, notwithstanding the infallible status of the teaching of the Ordinary Magisterium on this question (cf. reply to the *dubium* about the status of *Ordinatio Sacerdotalis* presented to the Congregation for the Doctrine of the Faith, October 28, 1995).

5

CEREMONIAL ACTIONS

5.1 Genuflections

In some places there are no genuflections during Mass or
when entering and leaving the church where the Blessed
Sacrament is reserved. Instead there may be a simple bow,
perhaps a curtsey. Is there a general law and perhaps particular laws by episcopal conferences about this?

The general law for the celebrant at Mass is precise. The
General Instruction of the Roman Missal, no. 233, states clearly:
"Three genuflections are made during Mass: after the showing of the eucharistic bread, after the showing of the chalice, and before communion. If there is a tabernacle with the
blessed sacrament in the sanctuary, a genuflection is made
before and after Mass and whenever anyone passes in front
of the blessed sacrament." Such a general law only applies
to those who are physically capable of genuflecting.

In some traditional cultures, for example in parts of Asia,
the most reverential human gesture is a profound bow,
and genuflecting may even have unpleasant connotations.
Therefore, several episcopal conferences, with the permission of the Holy See, have changed the genuflection to a
deep bow. It is to be noted that people who are part of these
traditional cultures are not only familiar with the meaning
of a deep bow in civil and religious circumstances, but they

also know exactly how to make it, graciously, without haste and with a sense of prayer.

However, outside these countries with a particular law, no priest can take it upon himself to substitute a bow for a genuflection during Mass or when passing before the Blessed Sacrament or when entering or leaving a sanctuary in which the tabernacle is located. I assume you are speaking of such behavior—which constitutes a grave abuse.

Some priests may argue that genuflecting when celebrating Mass "facing the people" looks ungainly. They may even claim that this is why the *multiple* genuflections of the old rite were eliminated in the postconciliar reform of the liturgy. However, the three mandatory genuflections in the modern rite were intended to be a simplification that invites the celebrant to carry out this gracious act of adoration and humility without haste, reverently and in a spirit of interior prayer. The genuflection was meant to be emphasized, not abolished. It would appear that this desired effect was not accomplished. Therefore I would hope to see some more genuflections added to the rite of Mass at certain relevant points.

Your question also raises the question of the regrettable trend of the laity no longer genuflecting. At first they substitute a bow, or a trivial curtsey, for the genuflection, but soon this is replaced by a nod of the head, and finally there is no act of respect at all. Some people follow the bad example of misguided clergy. Others act out of ignorance. Whatever the cause, the answer to such a trend is a strong spiritual catechesis on our faithful response to the Real Presence of Jesus Christ. This catechesis seems pastorally preferable to brusque attempts to "correct" people or only to proclaim the general law, set out above.

The first group that needs to be catechized in eucharistic reverence is made up of those who carry out liturgical ministries: the servers and lectors, choir, cantors, musicians, ushers, sacristans, and so forth. Lectors and cantors who come from the body of the church to the ambo, or a singing lectern, in the sanctuary need to be reminded that they are only permitted to substitute a bow for the genuflection if they have some disability. Children in particular need to be taught the meaning of genuflecting and how to do it well.

5.2 *When and Where to Genuflect*

In some churches it is difficult to know when and where to genuflect. For example, when servers pass behind the freestanding altar and a tabernacle is located at the back of that sanctuary, should they bow to the altar or genuflect to the tabernacle?

The example you provide can easily be resolved in the light of the general law (cf. *General Instruction of the Roman Missal*, no. 233). It is clear that the Eucharist takes precedence over the altar; therefore, the server genuflects to Our Lord in the tabernacle. However, if he passes behind the altar after the Consecration, he genuflects to the Eucharist on the altar.

If a liturgical procession, moving, for example, from the sacristy to the sanctuary, passes the Blessed Sacrament chapel, no reverence is made to the Blessed Sacrament (cf. *Ceremonial of Bishops*, no. 71). But individual persons passing that chapel should genuflect. If the tabernacle is located to one side of the altar, but in or very close to the sanctuary, it would suffice that the clergy and servers only genuflect toward the tabernacle on arriving and when leaving the sanctuary for a Mass or other celebration.

5.3 The Double Genuflection?

Is the double genuflection now prohibited? Many people still make it.

The new directives for eucharistic adoration did not maintain the double genuflection (kneeling on both knees for a moment while bowing the head) as universal practice before the Blessed Sacrament exposed (cf. *Eucharistic Worship outside Mass*, no. 84). While the clergy may be aware of this and some insist on reminding people not to make the double genuflection, many of the faithful often continue to make this extra act of reverence, and this applies not only to older people who have been accustomed to make it since childhood. Nevertheless, the double genuflection could be restored in any country by a decision of the episcopal conference. In Australia, the bishops decided to retain the double genuflection, and Rome confirmed their decision, so it is still required in that country.

No one should ever be discouraged from making this extra act of reverence to Our Lord. That would be as pastorally insensitive as forbidding people to make small gestures that are ethnic religious customs. The rationale for eliminating the double genuflection seems to have been to avoid any distinction between acts of reverence to Our Lord present in the tabernacle or the monstrance. Like certain other modifications, it seemed reasonable at the time, but experience has proved that in fact it diminished devotion and reverence. As already noted, some replace genuflecting to the Eucharist with a bow, and even that reverence is eventually replaced by—nothing at all. In an era when we desperately need to recover a sense of the sacred, not only in word but in action, it is to be hoped that other episcopal conferences will follow the Australian example and restore the double genuflection. It might also serve as reparation for much irreverence and indifference toward Our Lord in the Holy Eucharist.

5.4 Liturgical Dancing?

Is liturgical dancing permitted during Mass?

This short question opens the whole problem of appropriate inculturation, and there can be no brief answer to it. I believe that the best approach would be to make a clear distinction between *liturgical dancing* in the West and *religious dancing* in other cultures in the wider world.

1. Let us begin in the West. In 1975, there was a negative reply to your question from the then Sacred Congregation for the Sacraments and Divine Worship, *Dance in the Liturgy*. The profane and erotic elements in dancing in the West were cited, and the distracting nature of this dancing and its worldly associations were adduced as a strong reason against it.

This reply was a reaction against the fad of liturgical dancing in the seventies, which continued in some places during the eighties. I well recall various attempts at liturgical dancing in those years. Some were incongruous, even embarrassing, for example, when a gowned youth was surrounded by swaying damsels just after Communion and at the jubilee Mass of a very embarrassed elderly bishop. But I have also seen this dancing carried out well, for example, children trained to dance reverently and wave palms in a Palm Sunday procession. Back in the seventies, one of France's well-known liturgists promoted a skilled professional dancer who obviously prayed through her every gesture and movement. These last examples did not take place *during* Mass. But the issue is neither skill nor aesthetic quality. Something has "gone wrong" here, and this makes many people feel uncomfortable when they see liturgical dancing. So we have to ask deeper questions that go beyond whether this is permitted according to liturgical law.

In Western society we should ask an initial question: *What is liturgical dancing meant to convey?* Our habit of *watching* someone dance, the ballet tradition, seems to cause problems once dancing enters worship. The liturgical dance becomes a spectacle. Is this meant to teach us, to inspire us —or to entertain us? When it ends with applause, it has obviously entertained us. It may have been done well, or, as I also recall, it may have involved the children of admiring mothers! But that applause shows that it is not liturgical. This presentation has become a form of religious ballet, a show, an item on the program. This dancing may find a legitimate place in religious theatre, such as a medieval mystery play, but not within the action of the Mass.

We may therefore ask a more basic question: *What is liturgical dancing meant to do?* Here we need to take account of the modern crisis of Christian worship, which largely revolves around a disastrous overstatement of the instructional dimension of worship. This problem still plagues us —words and more words, the altar turned into a pulpit, the personality cult of the "presider", trite songs and rationed silence. Therefore it is interesting, and not surprising, that liturgical dancing spread in the West at the very time when ceremonial and ritual actions were being rejected and when language came to dominate Catholic worship.

Here I would honor the intentions of some who promoted liturgical dancing in the unfortunate years of "ex-

perimentation" and desacralization. They at least were trying to resacralize the liturgy by giving it back some sense of
movement and ceremony. They knew that ceremonial is a
specific religious spectacle where watching *can be* active participation. I believe they were trying to fill the vacuum left
by stripped sanctuaries and Masses reduced to talk shows.
One only had to listen to the rationale they presented to
justify their dancing. Some described the movements of the
old High Mass as a "solemn holy dance", and there is some
wisdom in that unusual perception. But when the argument
shifted to the "dancing altar boys of Seville" or the swaying
Shakers, this seemed to be appealing to obscure exceptions
to set up a general rule.

Putting it simply, *religious* dance is not a normal part of
Western culture, and thus "liturgical dancing" should find
no place in the celebration of Mass and the sacraments. This
is not to exclude it absolutely from religious experience. In
a reverent and skilled form, it may be appropriate in a para-
liturgy, in religious theatre and at grand outdoor events, such
as eucharistic congresses. But within the eucharistic celebration, the ceremonial itself, the gestures, reverences and pro-
cessions, make up our sacred "dance before the Lord".

2. When we turn to the wider Church, beyond the West,
we find cultures where traditions of religious dance pre-
date evangelization. This is where dancing in worship seems
"natural", hence we should cease calling it "liturgical dancing". It is religious dancing. In these countries in recent
decades, Christian religious dancing or movement, such as
swaying and rhythmic clapping, has become well established,
and it is regulated by the competent authorities, the local
Ordinary and the episcopal conference. But I would underline a major difference between this appropriate inculturation and what happened in the West. This is real *religious*

dance, and the people often spontaneously *take part* in it.

I was particularly impressed by participatory religious dancing at the procession of gifts during some liturgies celebrated in Kenya and by the rhythmic movements of the people during the procession of the gifts in Ghana— a procession involving the whole congregation. This was a participatory activity, not an entertaining spectacle or performance with self-conscious overtones. This activity does not come under most of the strictures of the 1975 ruling from the Sacred Congregation for Divine Worship and the Sacraments.

Therefore, in 1994, in the *Instruction on Inculturation and the Roman Liturgy*, from the same Congregation, we find that dancing may be incorporated into the liturgy where dance is an inherent part of the culture of the people and is "not simply a performance". This activity may even be promoted in places where dancing has a religious meaning compatible with Christianity. This cultural context accounts for the positive approach various episcopal conferences have taken to the question. But, the same conferences and other authorities have pointed out that even in traditional cultures a blanket approval for all forms of dance during worship must be avoided. Some dances and gestures from pre-Christian traditions relate to cults or the worship of false gods, even demons, not to mention the erotic overtones of some dances that would also exclude them from Catholic worship. Borrowing from another religious culture, for example Hinduism, may also raise problems of catechetical confusion or even syncretism. But when actions and gestures have wider cultural meanings, the Church can surely appropriate them, just as she has done over the two millennia of her glorious history.

Therefore, to sum up an answer to this simple question, liturgical dancing should not take place during Mass in Western societies, where dancing in such a context is not part of the culture. However Christian religious dance may be appropriate, even praiseworthy, in those cultures where it is part of the cultural patrimony and where it is regulated by the Ordinary and the episcopal conference.

5.5 *Incense at Mass*

> I believe incense can be used at any Mass. In the past it was only used at Solemn Mass or a *Missa cantata*.

Incense can be used at any Mass (*General Instruction of the Roman Missal*, no. 235; *Ceremonial of Bishops*, no. 86). The intention behind this widening of the use of incense is obviously to promote the more frequent use of this rich sign of prayer and sanctification. However, it would seem preferable to use incense only when there is some music at Mass, because the incensing of the altar and gifts is best carried out during singing or music. In the past, incense was seen in many parishes only at Benediction and funerals. Today it should normally be used at the principal sung Mass on all Sundays and solemnities. Not only the thurifer but also the celebrant and deacon should be trained in how to use the thurible graciously and correctly.

5.6 *Incense at Exposition and Benediction*

> When is it necessary to use incense at exposition of the Blessed Sacrament followed by Benediction?

Incense does not have to be used at the beginning of "simple exposition", when the *ciborium* is set on the altar, but it may be used. However, for the solemn form of exposition, when the *monstrance* is set on the altar or on a throne, incense should be used at the beginning of exposition. During the rite of Benediction, incense *must* be used, that is, when the eucharistic blessing is given with the monstrance. Its use is optional when Benediction is given with a ciborium.

5.7 *Incense without a Server*

> It seems awkward to use incense when there is no server at Benediction or funerals. Is it lawful to use the little stand from which the thurible can hang while incense is put in it?

The stand is a practical solution for such a situation. It is lawful and, if it is arranged carefully, with practice, using incense in this way need not seem awkward. These stands may also be equipped with a bar over which the humeral veil is draped at Benediction or with a ledge for the holy water vessel and sprinkler at funerals. But it must be admitted that no celebrant finds it easy to put a humeral veil on himself. Therefore, here we are not describing an ideal or normal situation, and it follows that some effort should be made to have servers assisting at the gracious rites of adoring our Eucharistic Lord and at the celebration of Christian funerals.

5.8 *Bowls of Burning Incense*

> I saw bowls of burning incense brought up in procession during one Mass I attended. Is that allowed?

Outside an appropriate cultural context, this is a pointless innovation, because we already have a gracious liturgical way of offering incense. To me it seems theatrical and contrived. Some have promoted it, associated with liturgical dancing.

The predominant Christian liturgical tradition is to burn incense in a thurible, that is, a metal bowl with a perforated cover that hangs from chains. There are several exceptions. When an altar is dedicated, after it has been anointed with Chrism, a brazier may be set upon it and incense or aromatic gums are burned in it. This is a sign of the Sacrifice of Christ that will be celebrated here and the sweetness of the prayers of Christ's faithful, rising with that one acceptable Sacrifice. In the Apocalypse an angel takes a "golden censer" and offers "the prayers of the saints" as incense before the throne of God (cf. Revelation 8:3–4). Alternatively, five crosses made of small candles or tapers may be placed on the five consecration crosses that are carved into the top (mensa) of the altar. Incense grains are placed on these before they are lit, and the incense is burned into the five crosses. Braziers also appear in the ancient Rite of Lyons. In the Christian East incense is sometimes burned at home in a small standing thurible, which is kept near the family ikons.

Something similar to what you describe might be authorized by an episcopal conference, with the approval of the Holy See, but only because this way of offering incense is already part of the local culture.

6

DURING THE LITURGY
OF THE WORD

6.1 *Greeting the Assembly Twice*

> In some parishes the celebrant says "Good morning" at
> the beginning of Mass. Is this allowed?

This well-intentioned mistake is really as strange as greeting someone twice! The real greeting of the people is *already* contained in a sacred liturgical formula, one of the
Christian greetings drawn from the Scriptures or tradition,
such as "The Lord be with you" or "The grace of our Lord
Jesus Christ . . .", eliciting a response from the people. This
greeting is also a kind of blessing, a mutual recognition of
the presence of the Holy Spirit in both celebrant and people
and the wish that this divine presence would abide forever.
To add "Good morning" to these great Christian greetings
is thus at least a kind of superfluous repetition. But it also
reveals a failure to understand the deeper meaning of the
sacred greetings in the liturgy.

In celebrating the liturgy, we adopt different forms of
language and expression from those we would normally use
in daily life, precisely to distinguish this holy assembly from
other gatherings or meetings. We address one another with
a new language, as God's Priestly People, the baptized, confirmed and ordained members of the Mystical Body. In this

sacred time we are caught up in the sublime action of the Lord's Sacrifice, and each Christian plays his role according to the permanent consecration received in the character sacraments. But this is deeper than "role playing". The way we relate to each other during the liturgy describes truth and reality: first, that we are a consecrated People; then, the further reality that the priest has been consecrated to act "in Persona Christi" when he celebrates the Lord's Sacrifice; and, ultimately, that we are all being called in the earthly liturgy to share in the eternal worship of the Holy Trinity in heaven. The biblical and liturgical greetings thus recognize the presence of Jesus Christ in us, which is the prerequisite for His presence in the proclaimed word and for His real and substantial presence in the Eucharist (cf. *General Instruction of the Roman Missal*, no. 7).

I described saying "Good morning" as a well-intentioned mistake because usually it is motivated by a priestly desire to be warm and pastoral (even though the celebrant can easily draw people into the celebration through the words he chooses to introduce the Mass). However, adding a secular greeting to the liturgy may reveal another agenda—secularizing the way we worship. Those who still want to secularize worship intrude mundane comments and actions into the rite. They should be gently reminded that in fact they are living in the recent past, when that approach was in fashion, in the years when we heard about "religionless Christianity" in the "secular city" or, *pace* feminists, "modern man coming of age". But the Church has moved on beyond such theories, which did not arise within her ranks, and so surprisingly enough has the world around us. Really "reading the signs of the times" is full of surprises.

6.2 *The Alleluia Verse*

Is the Alleluia before the Gospel obligatory? Some priests
leave it out.

The Alleluia or, in Lent, the verse before the Gospel may
be omitted when it is not sung (cf. *General Instruction of the
Roman Missal*, no. 39). The *Introduction* to the *Lectionary for
Mass*, no. 23, says that it must be sung and that all should
take part in the singing. This should encourage us to sing
it at all Masses, for the beautiful melodies are easy to learn.

6.3 *Using the Book of the Gospels*

When and how is the Book of the Gospels to be used
during the liturgy?

The Book of the Gospels may be used at any celebration of
the Mass. The priorities would be as follow: (a) It must *always*
be used at a Solemn Mass, when there is a deacon and/or
concelebrants, in particular when the bishop presides. (b) It
should be used at any Mass when a deacon assists. (c) It may
be used at a Mass, for example on Sundays, when a reader
and servers assist the celebrant, in which case the reader
carries it in the procession to the altar. (d) It may be used
at celebrations of the Liturgy of the Hours (Divine Office)
when a Gospel reading is included in the rite. (e) Because
it has a further use in the sacramental rite, it must be used
at the ordination of bishops and deacons.

The Book of the Gospels is used during Mass according
to the following procedures. Before Mass, the appropriate
Gospel reading is marked with the ribbon. The deacon, or

if there is no deacon, a concelebrant, or lacking these, a reader, carries the book in the entrance procession. A deacon or concelebrant carrying the book comes immediately before the concelebrants or the celebrant, walking alone. It should be carried in both hands in a slightly raised way, but without being held too high, and it is never waved from side to side. Anyone carrying this book does not genuflect or bow on arriving at the sanctuary (for this sacred object is a symbol of Christ). The one carrying the book goes directly to the altar and places it at the center of the mensa (surface of the altar), if necessary, closer to the side from which it will later be taken for the procession to the ambo.

While the Alleluia verse is being sung, the deacon, concelebrant or celebrant who is to read the Gospel goes to the altar, that is, (a) after any incense has been prepared and blessed at the chair and (b) after he has been blessed or after he has said the private prayer. The book is then reverently taken from the altar and carried in procession to the ambo. It is placed on the ambo and carefully opened. If incense is used, the book is incensed with three double swings, to the center, the left and the right (cf. *Ceremonial of Bishops*, no. 74). The incensations take place after the words "A reading from. . . ."

The book rests on the ambo during the Gospel, and the deacon or priest reads the text with his hands joined, palm to palm, as usual. During the Gospel all present turn toward the ambo. At the end of the Gospel the deacon or priest sings or says, "This is the Gospel of the Lord" ("The Gospel of the Lord" in the U.S.), then, if a bishop presides, the deacon or priest normally takes the open book to him at the cathedra, so he can kiss it.

After the Gospel has been proclaimed, the Book of the Gospels may be left at the ambo or, preferably, taken by a server to the credence table. If it has been brought to the bishop to be kissed, the deacon or a server then takes it to the credence table. This book should always be treated with the greatest respect and *never* left on a seat or, worse, on the ground, leaning against a wall. In some places, it is carried back to the sacristy in the final procession. This is the practice in St. Peter's Basilica and has much to commend it. But this may also imply that incense should be used in the final procession to honor the book. Apart from the final procession in the Mass of the Chrism, I do not think that it is a necessary or normal practice to carry a smoking thurible in the final procession, even if this practice is customary in some places.

6.4 *The Order of the Gospel Procession*

Should the candle bearers and thurifer precede the deacon to the ambo, in procession, when he is not carrying the Book of the Gospels?

It has been argued that the incense and lights honor the Book of the Gospels, a symbol of Jesus Christ the living Word, and they are not carried in honor of the humble deacon! This is correct. I would only tolerate the procession without the book to avoid the sloppy ceremonial of candle bearers and thurifer meeting the deacon at the ambo. However, the issue is easily resolved by *always* using the Book of the Gospels if there is to be a Gospel procession. In churches where the altar, chair and ambo are very close to one another, the Book of the Gospels should be carried the longer way around the altar to make this "procession" a significant liturgical action.

6.5 Raising the Book of the Gospels?

Should the deacon or priest who reads the Gospel lift up the Book of the Gospels (or a lectionary) while singing or saying "(This is) the Gospel of the Lord"? This is quite widespread today.

It is argued that the statement "(This is) the Gospel of the Lord" combined with such a gesture falsely suggests that the book itself is the word of the Lord. This practice is not mentioned in any of the current official directives. Perhaps the American abbreviation of the words, which will no doubt become universal, somewhat weakens any identification of the Gospel of Christ with a book. It should be noted, however, that only the Pope may bless the assembly with the Book of the Gospels, after the Gospel has been read.

6.6 Lay People Reading the Gospel and Preaching

May a lay person read the Gospel or give the homily at Mass?

1. At Mass, the proclamation of the Gospel belongs first to the deacon, if he is assisting, then to the priest celebrant, when there is no deacon present. A bishop celebrating Mass may not read the Gospel when there is a deacon or priest assisting him. A lay person may not read the Gospel at Mass, but laity may act as lectors and read the other reading(s) and lead the responsorial psalm. Laity may also read the intentions of the General Intercessions. On the other hand, where necessary, lay readers may take part in the reading of the Passion on Palm Sunday and Good Friday.

2. Only a priest or deacon may preach a homily at Mass (cf. Canon 767 §1). The preaching of the word is part of the gift and mission of Holy Orders. On June 20, 1987, the Commission for the Authentic Interpretation of the Code of Canon Law (since 1988, the Pontifical Council for the Interpretation of Legislative Texts) reaffirmed Canon 767 §1 and stated that the local diocesan bishop does not have the power to dispense from this law. The *Instruction on Certain Questions Regarding the Collaboration of the Non-Ordained Faithful in the Sacred Ministry of Priests* (jointly published by eight Vatican departments in 1997), applies the same Canon in the section, Practical Provisions, Article 3. However, under special circumstances, a lay person or a male or female religious could read a prepared address or message, after a brief homily given by the celebrant or deacon or before the final blessing. The bishop may authorize this, for example, during a Sunday set aside for a special appeal or to promote a good cause such as the pro-life movement. Lay persons, such as catechists, or religious may also be permitted to read a homily when they are authorized to lead a Sunday Communion service in the absence of a priest. The text is usually prepared beforehand by or in consultation with a priest.

6.7 *Omitting the Creed*

Some priests leave out the Creed on Sundays. Is that an option?

The celebrant has no authority to omit the Profession of Faith at Sunday Mass or on the solemnities, when it is not optional. The Creed *may* also be said or sung on other appropriate occasions (cf. *General Instruction of the Roman Missal*, no. 44).

One wonders why some priests omit the Creed. It is at least imprudent. They may leave themselves open to unjust accusations of a "lack of faith", and so on. But perhaps some priests believe that the language of the Nicene Creed is too complex for the faithful to understand, as if any of us can ever fully comprehend, in this life, the truths of the Faith. Moreover, it is the priest's duty to catechize the faithful in the truths we profess in the creeds of the Church. On the other hand, if the only problem with reciting the Creed is a certain monotony, then it should be sung by everyone. However, I am still looking for a good vernacular musical version of the Creed that could be sung with conviction by the whole assembly.

6.8 Alternatives to the Creed

> I was present at a Mass when they used a creed I had never heard before. Are there any alternatives to the Creed?

There are some official alternatives to the Nicene Creed that may be used during Mass.

1. Episcopal conferences may permit saying the Apostles' Creed as an option at Sunday Mass. From a catechetical point of view, this may be useful, because it ensures that the faithful, especially children, learn our ancient baptismal creed. But from a liturgical point of view, it is not within the classical liturgical tradition of saying or singing the great conciliar Creed of the Councils of Nicaea and Constantinople.

2. At all Masses on Easter Sunday, the Creed may be replaced by the Renewal of Baptismal Promises. Then the faithful are sprinkled with blessed Easter water. This gives everyone a chance to celebrate the sacramental meaning of the Paschal Mystery, even if they did not take part in the Easter Vigil.

3. At the Easter Vigil Mass and the Ritual Masses for Baptism and Confirmation, the Creed is omitted because the Profession of Faith has been made in the baptismal promises.

However, I suspect that you heard one of those home-made "creeds" apparently used in some dissenting circles. These compositions are never permitted because they are not the authentic and authoritative expression of the faith of the Catholic Church. The *Catechism of the Catholic Church* (nos. 167, 185–97, 512, 815, 1816) explains the reason we have creeds and what they embody. They express the one faith that secures the unity of the Church. They express our shared faith, "we believe", which is my personal faith—"I believe".

I suppose some people compose their own creeds, not necessarily because they presume to improve on the truth the Church professes, but because they are trying to make the content of the Creed more intelligible. They would argue that we do not understand all the words in the Nicene Creed. That may be true. But, as I have remarked, the revealed Mysteries of our faith are never fully comprehensible in this life, where we are pilgrims, where we do not yet know and see our loving God face to face. Moreover, those rolling metaphysical phrases at the beginning of the Nicene Creed were hammered out in ecumenical councils of the Church, precisely to maintain and protect the central truths of the Holy Trinity and the Incarnation. On the other hand, some composed "creeds" include heresies or trivia. After reciting vapid nonsense about trees and flowers, or about some New Age "god within me", or, worse still, renaming the Holy Trinity to satisfy gender feminists, it would be a lie to say aloud, or in one's heart, "This is our faith! This is the faith of the Church! We are proud to profess it in Christ Jesus our Lord!" But, with joy and trust, that is exactly what the great creeds of Holy Church invite us to proclaim.

6.9 General Intercessions on Weekdays

Is the "Prayer of the Faithful" obligatory at weekday Mass? When is it required?

The *General Instruction of the Roman Missal*, no. 45, says that "it is appropriate that this prayer be included in all Masses celebrated with a congregation." In practice, the "Prayer of the Faithful" (preferably described as the *General Intercessions*) is a normal part of the Mass on all Sundays and solemnities. The General Intercessions would be appropriate on major feasts and memorials. But these prayers are not obligatory at every weekday Mass. For reasons of time —for example, when commuters assist at Mass—they are often omitted.

However, as with a succinct comment on the readings or the saint of the day, there is much to commend including a *short* form of the General Intercessions in each weekday Mass. There are books available that provide good sets of intercessions for weekdays. Some priests adapt the intercessions provided in the breviary for Morning Prayer (Lauds) and Evening Prayer (Vespers), although the *petitions* in these prayers are not the same as the *intentions* envisaged for the General Intercessions at Mass. The complete texts of these breviary intercessions, including the Our Father, could only be used on occasions when the major hours are fully incorporated into the Mass (for this procedure, see *Ceremonies of the Modern Roman Rite*, nos. 765–73).

Lacking a set text, the celebrant could improvise a simple form of the General Intercessions in the following way. He introduces the intentions with one short sentence, always addressed to the people, for example, "Let us bring our prayers before God our loving Father." Then he provides several short intentions, preferably using the simplest of the three options for the intentions, for example: "For those who suffer from anxiety or fear; Let us pray to the Lord. . . ." Note that these are *intentions*. They are not petitions addressed directly to God, beginning "O Lord. . . ." The prayer is the petition or silent prayer, made in response to "Let us pray to the Lord" (cf. *General Instruction*, no. 47). The celebrant concludes the intercessions by extending his hands and offering a simple prayer with the short ending, for example, "Almighty God, our Father, you know all our needs. Accept these prayers we confidently make, through Christ our Lord. Amen."

In a community with a tradition of intercessory prayer, members of the congregation may add their own spontaneous intentions at a weekday Mass. However, they should be trained not to turn intentions into long prayers addressed to God—or, worse still, into thinly veiled exhortations directed at other people! But the shortest and simplest form, favored above, excludes the possibility of descending into preaching or pious verbosity.

For a detailed study of the "Prayer of the Faithful", readers may wish to consult the introduction to a work I edited: *Let Us Pray to the Lord*, published by E.J. Dwyer (Sydney and New York: Costello, 1984).

7

DURING THE LITURGY
OF THE EUCHARIST

7.1 *Preparing the Altar*

When visiting churches in Southern Europe, I noticed
that the chalice, missal and even the cruets are all arranged on the altar at the beginning of Mass. The celebrant seems to stay at the altar for most of the Mass.
He even preaches there in some parishes. In the U.S. and
Central Europe, on the other hand, the vessels and missal
are brought to the altar in the course of the celebration,
and the celebrant uses the chair and the lectern as well
as the altar. Are both practices correct?

No. The practice in the U.S. and Central Europe is in accord with the post-Vatican II Roman Rite. The other practice constitutes a serious failure to understand the role of
the altar, ambo and chair in the various stages of the celebration of Mass.

Except for the cloth (an antependium, if used), the cross,
candles and perhaps flowers, nothing else is meant to be
on or around the altar at the beginning of a Mass celebrated with the people. The chalice, the missal and its stand
or cushion and the ewer, bowl and towel should all be on
the credence table. The cruets and paten(s) and/or ciboria

should be at the table of gifts, for the procession of the gifts, or on the credence table if there is no procession.

Having kissed (and incensed) the altar, the celebrant goes to the chair to begin Mass. He does not return to the altar to read from the missal during the Liturgy of the Word, nor should he ever preach at the altar, because it is not a pulpit. The ambo or lectern is the place for the readings and, normally, for preaching. When the celebrant is presiding from the chair, a server holds the book before him for the preparatory rites, Opening Prayer, Creed and General Intercessions. The celebrant goes to the altar *after* the missal, corporal and chalice have been placed there by a server or servers. He usually returns to the chair for the Prayer after Communion and the blessing, although he may choose to remain at the altar. A small lectern placed near the chair may be tolerated when no server is available to hold the missal.

7.2 *One Prayer for Offering Bread and Wine*

I noted that a priest offered the bread and wine together in a single action. Is this permissible?

I presume that he said "Blessed are you, Lord God of all creation . . ." once, adapting the words and raising both paten and chalice. This is probably done to save time or to simplify the preparation of the gifts. It is not permissible. It is interesting, however, to note that this is the practice in Masses celebrated according to the traditional Dominican and Carmelite Rites. But here there is a logical reason for it. The paten and the chalice containing wine and water have already been prepared by the celebrant at the credence table just before Mass, similar to what the celebrant does in the Byzantine Rite at the table of prothesis. Therefore the gifts come to the altar, as it were, prepared, and it seems logical to offer them together with one prayer during the offertory. But we do not do that in the modern Roman Rite, nor was it the practice in the preconciliar Roman Rite.

Even if some chalices have been prepared on the credence table before Mass, as may happen during a major concelebration, for instance, there are always two distinct but similar prayers and actions for separately offering the bread and wine. There is no obligation to say these prayers aloud, indeed, the first option is to say them quietly, whether or not singing or music accompany these actions. There is much to be said for that option because it eliminates a certain repetitive element that no doubt has also influenced some priests to say "Blessed are you, Lord God of all creation . . ." only once.

7.3 *Omitting the Washing of the Hands*

Is the washing of the hands optional? One priest in our parish no longer does it. He says, "My hands are clean so I don't need to wash them again."

The washing of hands is not optional, and it has nothing to do with cleaning dirty hands. This is why it still takes place even when there has been an earlier washing of hands, for example, when the bishop has already cleansed the Chrism from his hands at a Confirmation Mass or when the celebrant washed his hands after imposing blessed ashes on Ash Wednesday. The washing of hands at the preparation of the gifts is a symbolic ritual act, hence the beautiful penitential prayer that accompanies it, asking the Lord to ". . . wash away my iniquity" to "cleanse me of my sin." The outward purification of these anointed hands that will soon hold the Host and Chalice is a sign of the inner purity of the priestly soul, the single-hearted purity of intention to which every priest is called as he serves and enters the eucharistic mysteries of the Holy Trinity.

One need not go so far as to impute desacralization to priests who omit the washing of hands. They may regard the liturgical washing of hands as only dipping fingers in a bowl of water or allowing a few drops of water to trickle over their thumbs. Who could blame them for seeing this as a rather trivial action that might be omitted? But they should be invited to consider adopting a fuller sign, that is, washing their *hands* without haste, using a larger jug and basin, not a small water cruet and a dish, and then drying the hands with a towel that is ample and practical, not a mere square of linen. This was and is the practice at pontifical ceremonies, where the bishop's ewer and basin are also meant to be significant vessels of precious metal.

7.4 *Congregation Standing during the Eucharistic Prayer*

In some parishes the people stand for the whole of the Eucharistic Prayer. Is this permitted?

No. The *General Instruction of the Roman Missal*, no. 21, says that the people "should kneel at the consecration unless prevented by the lack of space, the number of people present, or some other good reason". The exceptions could include a Mass celebrated outdoors or in a hall or stadium where it would be difficult to kneel, but in that situation at least the deacons and servers are still obliged to kneel for the Consecration. The precise extent of kneeling during the Eucharistic Prayer varies from country to country, according to rules laid down by each episcopal conference.

However, a destructive tendency is evident in some places, that is, *the deliberate attempt to abolish all kneeling at Mass.* Certain liturgists have raised specious arguments against kneeling at Mass, particularly during the Eucharistic Prayer. It is claimed that kneeling is only a penitential act—ignoring its dimension of adoration. It is claimed that we stand when someone important enters a room—ignoring the fact that we kneel and genuflect before our God. It is claimed that only standing is a pure and ancient liturgical posture—ignoring centuries of practice in the West in favor of some kneeling during Mass. In certain instances, the local culture is invoked to justify a ban on kneeling. But balanced inculturation also includes respect for the spiritual elements that Christianity brings to an existing culture. Furthermore, we cannot ignore the scriptural warrant for kneeling, for example: Luke 22:41; Acts 9:40, 20:36, 21:5.

The same liturgists who campaign to abolish kneeling at the Consecration also oppose kneeling after receiving Communion. One can only wonder at their real motives. Kneelers have even been removed from some churches to force the people to stand or sit. In the face of this threat to the freedom of the faithful and their traditions of devotion, priests should defend the continuity of our tradition, the popular piety of our people, and a pastoral point that seems to have been forgotten—the right of children, infirm and short people to be visually involved in the most sacred moments of the liturgy.

7.5 *Changing the Words of Consecration*

Can a priest alter the words of consecration? If he does so, is the Eucharist invalidated?

No priest may presume to alter the words of consecration. The prescribed words are set out in each of the Eucharistic Prayers, with slight variations in the accompanying text. Furthermore, the common form for consecrating the Eucharist in all the Eucharistic Prayers was specified by Pope Paul VI in the Apostolic Constitution *Missale Romanum*, promulgating the new Roman Missal, April 3, 1969. This may be found at the front of the altar edition of the missal. Acting as the "supreme authority", the Pope approved and defined what pertains to the validity of a sacrament (cf. Canon 841). Of course, the words of consecration in the Roman Canon of the preconciliar Missal of St. Pius V and in the Canons of other traditional Western and Eastern Rites remain both valid and licit.

The second question depends on how the priest alters the words. In turn, this depends on the opinions of two schools of theologians and canonists as to what words constitute the *essential* form for consecrating the Eucharist. The first school argues that the essential words are "This is my body" and "This is . . . my blood", hence once these words denoting transubstantiation are said, the Eucharist is validly confected.

However, a second school of thought has argued that the other words expressing the New Covenant and the finality of the Eucharistic Sacrifice are also essential for validity. This second view was invoked in the mischievous debate orchestrated some years ago by certain traditionalists over the words *pro multis*, "for many", that are translated in

English and some other modern languages as "for all". On historical grounds I would regard insisting on these words as an untenable position, because in fact they are lacking in the Eucharistic Prayers of some ancient rites.

Therefore, taking the first position, which favors the essential words denoting transubstantiation, I would argue that invalidity would only be possible if the priest were to change the *meaning* of those few essential words. For example, if the priest were to say, "This means my body", (as the Protestant scholar Moffat translated the New Testament) or "this symbolizes my body" or "this is the sign of my body", then this change would invalidate the Mass. However, were the priest illicitly to add some words of his own to the existing text, without changing the meaning of the essential words, the Mass would still be valid. Therefore, if a scrupulous priest were to say, in the vernacular, "for *many*" instead of "for all" or were a feminist priest to say "for you and for all *women and men*", these unauthorized and unnecessary changes would not affect the validity of the Mass. For the sake of scrupulous persons and following common sense, it should be noted that it seems difficult to invalidate a Mass when the words of consecration are said aloud and in the vernacular.

7.6 *Anticipating the Fraction*

> At a Protestant communion service I noticed that the minister broke the bread at the words of Our Lord, "He broke". Why don't our priests do this at Mass? It seems closer to the Last Supper in the Bible.

In fact this practice is not closer to the accounts of the Last Supper in the Synoptic Gospels of Matthew, Mark and Luke and in 1 Corinthians 11:23–26 (which may well be the earliest written account, passed on to St. Paul by the Jerusalem church). In the light of the Passover ritual, some scholars have reconstructed what happened as a sequence of acts at the Last Supper, but we are not bound to attempt to do this when we celebrate the Eucharist. The Church interprets the whole Last Supper action in her liturgies. She has placed the eucharistic words of Jesus Christ within the central act of the great thanksgiving prayer, or *anaphora*, so that these words of the Incarnate Word may effect the consecration of the bread and wine. But this moment is part of a wider framework that we call the eucharistic action.

The eucharistic action of our Roman Rite clearly and graciously extends what appears to take place in a few moments at the Last Supper. Therefore the Liturgy of the Eucharist unfolds in these four stages: (1) Jesus Christ *took bread and wine* (the preparation of the gifts); (2) He *gave thanks* and so blessed the bread and wine (the Eucharistic Prayer); (3) He *broke the bread* now transformed into His Body (the fraction); (4) He *gave* His Body and Blood to the apostles (the Communion Rite). The *General Instruction of the Roman Missal*, no. 48, sets out the first three stages of this fourfold action.

In the uncertain years after Vatican II, a few priests took it upon themselves to break the bread at the words "he broke it". They may have meant well and probably did not know that long ago this had already crept into a few medieval rites, when the celebrant slightly tore the bread at these words. When the Roman Rite was standardized, in the "Tridentine Mass" of the Missal of St. Pius V (1570), the celebrant was instructed to break the Host only during the embolism "Libera nos . . .", which he said silently after the Lord's Prayer. This was modified in the revised rite of the Missal of Paul VI, in line with what liturgists had been suggesting for some years and returning to a more ancient Roman tradition. The fraction now takes place slightly later, that is, after the sign of peace and during the singing or saying of the Agnus Dei, "Lamb of God. . . ."

The fraction during the Agnus Dei seems to be a logical and beautiful development, and it allows time for breaking a larger Host into fragments. It also has a scriptural nuance, in accord with the Gospel of St. John. The sacred author tells us that Jesus was crucified when the Passover lambs were being sacrificed (cf. John 19:14). Broader biblical scholarship, open to archaeology, would accept John's Gospel as perhaps a more reliable guide to various historical details than the other Gospels. So by paradox, the current practice of breaking the Host(s) during the Agnus Dei is surely scriptural.

You mentioned that you saw this "breaking of bread" at a Protestant service. In the light of better ecumenical understanding, it is interesting to know how this came about. The Reformation practice you describe emerged in the Zwinglian and Calvinist communion rites, where the Eucharistic Prayer or Canon was abolished and replaced by a reading of the scriptural account of the Last Supper, during which the minister reenacted the action of Our Lord. This rested on the Protestant theology that the Eucharist is a meal in memory of the death of Christ, hence the Last Supper should be reenacted, like a little play with a narrative, that is, during the reading of some appropriate Scripture verses. In this perspective it is quite logical to break the bread at the words "He broke it".

The more radical Protestants strongly influenced Archbishop Thomas Cranmer, author of the second Anglican *Book of Common Prayer* (1552, revised in 1662). He also telescoped the action of the Last Supper into the words of institution, but at the end of a prayer of consecration. This was followed immediately by a communion rite. Later Anglican liturgists, including some renowned scholars, reacted against Cranmer. They recognized that this was not within the classical liturgical tradition. Some of them also admitted that Cranmer had completely rejected all Catholic eucharistic doctrine. Therefore they sought to recover the fraction rite *after* the consecration and before the communion rite. This sequence is to be found in most modern versions of the Anglican liturgies. Therefore I doubt that you were present at an Episcopalian service.

7.7 *Genuflecting at the Consecration*

Under normal circumstances, should the priest genuflect at the Consecration?

Yes. The missal clearly states that, after the elevation of the Host and the Chalice, the priest "genuflects in adoration". In the Latin original this is "genuflexus adorat", in the Missals of both Paul VI and St. Pius V. The Latin in fact emphasizes that the celebrant adores as he bends his knee before the Lord. Therefore, no priest has the authority to replace the genuflection with a bow or some other gesture. In our Roman Rite, genuflecting is mainly associated with an act of faith in the Real Presence of Jesus Christ in the Holy Eucharist. Therefore, after each elevation, the celebrant's genuflection is his affirmation before the community that Christ is now really present on the altar under the appearances of bread and wine.

The exceptions to this norm are obvious. A celebrant with a physical disability or an ailment, such as arthritis, would find genuflecting very difficult or painful. He might substitute a reverent bow for the genuflection. There is also the more obvious case, envisaged in Canon 930 §1, of priests who are unable to stand and who are permitted to celebrate Mass seated.

After the elevations, concelebrants bow deeply as the celebrant genuflects. When conditions oblige the people to stand during the Consecration, they might well be encouraged to bow when the celebrant genuflects. As noted elsewhere, this would not apply to attempts to force the people to stand when they could kneel in accord with liturgical law.

7.8 One Genuflection after the Elevations?

> In the seminary we were told that it is enough for the celebrant to genuflect once, after the elevation of the Chalice.

This is not correct. As a deliberate change in the normal procedure, it may even imply a curious eucharistic theology that the Real Presence is not completely "there" until both the bread and the wine have been consecrated. This may be a variation of the error that Christ is truly received only when one receives the Eucharist under both Species.

7.9 Deacon Standing at the Consecration

> At Mass, should the deacon kneel or stand during the Consecration?

The deacon should kneel at the Consecration. Unfortunately, in various places, even seminaries, deacons remain standing at the Consecration because the *General Instruction of the Roman Missal* was not clear on this point. But the *Ceremonial of Bishops*, no. 155, states that the deacon(s) ministering at the altar must kneel during the Consecration. The reason is simple: deacons are not concelebrants. They should kneel at the epiklesis and stand after the elevation of the Chalice, that is, after the celebrant genuflects, just before the acclamation. Before he kneels, the deacon removes the pall, if used, and uncovers any ciboria on the altar. Common sense indicates that the directive in the *Ceremonial of Bishops*, no. 155, is not restricted only to Masses celebrated by a bishop, because kneeling at the Consecration is an act of reverence to Our Lord, not to the bishop.

7.10 *The Memorial Acclamation*

> May the deacon say or sing, "Let us proclaim the mystery of faith" after the Consecration? This happens in a seminary chapel.

No. These words are strictly reserved to the celebrant of the Mass. Pope Paul VI made this clear in the Apostolic Constitution *Missale Romanum*, when he stated that the words "mysterium fidei" had been moved from the formula of consecrating the wine and were now to be said by the priest as an introduction to the acclamation made by the faithful. The rubrics for all the Eucharistic Prayers in the *Order of Mass* clearly indicate that the celebrant sings or says "mysterium fidei". Perhaps the practice of the deacon taking over this role has arisen because of the misleading ICEL version, "*Let us proclaim* the mystery of faith." This turns the words into the kind of invitation or exhortation that deacons make during the liturgy. But in fact "mysterium fidei" is a statement of fact: "This is the mystery of faith." The ICEL version also seems to draw our attention away from the Eucharist, with the result that the acclamation no longer seems to bear much relationship to the Eucharistic Mystery.

7.11 *Raising the Host at the Doxology*

At the "little elevation" I have noticed that some priests raise the Host on its edge above the paten while others leave the Host resting flat on the paten. What is correct?

First of all, let us never use the term "little elevation" to refer to the raising of the paten and the chalice at the doxology at the end of the Eucharistic Prayer. To understand what is behind the correct procedure, we need to make a distinction between an elevation that is a "showing" to the people and an elevation that is a sign of offering to God. There are four relevant moments in the liturgy that need to be understood in the light of this distinction: two acts of *offering* and two of *showing*.

1. At the preparation of the gifts or offertory, the paten is slightly raised but not "elevated" during the prayer "Blessed are you, Lord God of all creation. . . ." The bread remains on the paten as a sign that it is being set aside and thus *offered* to God, so that it may become the Body of Christ.

2. However, the elevation immediately after the Consecration is a solemn *showing* of the Host to the people for their adoration, and the words of the relevant rubric are the same as in the old missal: "Hostiam consecratam . . . osten-dit populo": he shows the consecrated Host to the people. Thus, it is not correct to leave the Host on the paten at

this elevation, for then the people cannot see it, nor would it be correct even to raise the paten beneath the Host, as is sometimes seen. Moreover, it is most important, especially in the modern situation, to take time over these elevations and to ensure that they are reverent and significant actions.

3. On the other hand, at the final doxology of the Eucharistic Prayer, we make a solemn sign of *offering* the Body and Blood of Christ to the Father in the Holy Spirit, as the magnificent text proclaims: "Through Him, with Him, in Him. . . ." Therefore the Host should remain on the paten and not be shown to the people. This action should also be a significant raising of the Body and Blood of the Lord, unlike the moderate gesture that was appropriate at the preparation of the gifts.

4. Before Holy Communion, the celebrant again *shows* the Host to the assembly. But this time he invites them to receive the Body of Christ, already broken so that it may be shared by the faithful. Nevertheless, the sacrificial imagery is also present in this gracious gesture of invitation. Jesus the Lamb of God has been broken in sacrifice for us. He is the slain Lamb, "Christ our Passover", given as Food for the blessed People of God who are now called to make their pilgrimage to his nuptial supper in eternity.

7.12 *Holding Hands during the Lord's Prayer?*

> In some parishes the people are encouraged to hold hands during the Our Father. Is this right?

Some religious movements, especially those promoting marriage and the family, favor holding hands during certain prayers. Having worked in that wonderful field for some years, I can understand their wish to affirm spousal love and family solidarity, especially in a world where these sacred realities are mocked and threatened. Therefore, there seems nothing wrong when a couple chooses to hold hands when praying the Our Father, even at Mass. It may also be the custom at home for members of a family to do this during grace at the table.

However, problems arise when *everyone* gathered in the church is expected to do this, because we know that there is no official liturgical directive for us all to do so. To encourage everyone to hold hands during the Our Father is an example of private or group piety intruding illicitly into public worship. One cannot impose a personal devotion, even something good.

The second point to consider is whether this practice is appropriate during the Lord's Prayer. As the *Catechism of the Catholic Church* (2777–865) explains, this greatest of prayers is an act of adoration of our transcendent Father, followed by seven petitions addressed to Him. This is why the celebrant extends his hands in praise and petition. But everyone "holding hands" does not reflect the meaning of this great prayer of adoration and petition. This is the wrong sign for this prayer because it is too "horizontal".

I would add the opinion that this is not just a question of what is right or wrong. At any moment during the liturgy, this practice seems unduly sentimental and hence not fitting. It can also be distracting and a source of embarrassment. When one steps outside the situation, a large crowd of people holding hands during formal worship looks plain silly.

7.13 *Extending Hands during the Lord's Prayer*

During the Our Father, some lay people are now holding their hands extended just like the priest. What is to be said of this practice?

This is quite a different matter from the question of "holding hands" during the Lord's Prayer. As you indicate, the celebrant is meant to extend his hands at this point in the Mass. Concelebrants are also instructed to hold their hands extended during the Our Father (cf. *Ceremonial of Bishops*, no. 159). I think there is nothing wrong if the people also choose to extend their hands during the Lord's Prayer. Because the practice is spreading in various places, and some children do it spontaneously, several episcopal conferences are enquiring whether Rome might authorize and encourage this gesture of adoration and petition among the faithful. This also marks a return to an early Christian custom. Frescoes in the Roman catacombs depict Christ's faithful with their hands raised in the *orantes* or *precantes* position.

7.14 *Not Singing the Lord's Prayer?*

Our diocesan liturgical office has announced that the Our Father should never be sung at Mass. Is that right?

This is just another fad, and I cannot find any intelligent reason for it. The Lord's Prayer sounds much better when the assembly sings it together, and let us never forget that St. Augustine said that we pray twice whenever we sing. There are beautiful musical settings for Our Lord's own prayer— so why remove this beauty from our worship? Moreover,

some musicologists claim that the familiar plainsong setting of the Lord's Prayer goes right back to the synagogue
and hence represents the most ancient of Christian musical traditions. I would not want to interfere in such a grand
Judaeo-Christian tradition. On the other hand, when someone proposes singing those repetitive and childish musical
settings of the Lord's Prayer dating from the sixties or seventies, it would be better to have the prayer said.

7.15 The Sign of Peace

Is the sign of peace always optional?

The sign of peace is optional, as indicated by the word "may"
in the *General Instruction of the Roman Missal*, no. 112, and
in the *Order of Mass*. However, this gracious Christian sign
is strongly recommended, and it is assumed that it will certainly take place at least on some occasions. It is clear that
it is to be given during the solemn celebration of Mass by
the bishop (cf. *Ceremonial of Bishops*, nos. 99–103). In line
with the continuity of our tradition, and consonant with
the bishop's liturgy, I would argue that it is obligatory at all
solemn eucharistic celebrations.

Therefore anyone who set out to abolish the sign of peace
would be acting against the norms of the Roman Rite. At
the same time, anyone who required it at *every* Mass could
be inadvertently undermining its value, as I learned myself
when I was a young priest. Soon after ordination, I was
very keen on promoting the sign of peace and invited the
sisters to exchange the sign at every early morning Mass
I celebrated in the parish convent. Eventually the superior
asked me to desist, at least at that early hour, when these

hard-working teaching sisters did not really want to start greeting one another. On a purely human level it was not pastorally appropriate in that situation.

Perhaps prejudice has arisen against the sign of peace because its importance has been exaggerated by some clergy, or because it has been imposed on people in an invasive way. There are reserved people who do not want to make body contact with others. Their freedom should be respected, but they should be encouraged at least to bow in a friendly way as they make their own form of the sign of peace.

Some lay enthusiasts who run around the church shaking everyone's hands have certainly undermined the meaning of the gesture. Unfortunately, the sign of peace may also become the occasion for boisterous behavior at children's Masses or an excuse for romantic behavior during youth Masses. Moreover, during the eucharistic celebrations of some religious movements, the prolonged sign of peace makes one wonder whether this is meant to be the high point of Christian liturgy. Nevertheless, these exaggerations can all be controlled and directed by patient catechesis. Simply because a liturgical action is at times carried out badly does not mean that it should be eliminated. That logic could be extended to many other good aspects of Catholic worship, with destructive effects.

7.16 Moving the Sign of Peace

> I have heard that the sign of peace may be moved to another place in the Mass. Is this advisable?

The question has been raised about moving the sign of peace to another part in the Rite of Mass. Liturgists have discussed moving it to after the penitential rite at the beginning of Mass or, more plausibly, to the moment where it is exchanged in the Ambrosian Rite of the Church of Milan, that is, just before the procession of the gifts. While this latter proposal would mark a departure from the venerable Roman tradition, it does make sense now that the sign of peace is exchanged by everyone and is no longer a formal "pax" passed along from the celebrant to the clergy and servers. The sign does seem to be somewhat disruptive in its present position before Holy Communion. If it preceded the procession of gifts, the sign of peace would also reflect the words of Our Lord: "First be reconciled to your brother, and then come and offer your gift" (Matthew 5:24). It would indicate a clear transition from the Liturgy of the Word to the Liturgy of the Eucharist, perhaps accompanied by a suitable antiphon or hymn. In some places, such music has already been illicitly introduced to accompany the sign of peace in its present position. While this is not envisaged in the Roman Rite, one can understand that this is also another attempt to cover the action and restore tranquility, dignity and meaning to it.

7.17 *How to Make the Sign of Peace*

Is there a "correct" way of making the sign of peace.

The episcopal conference decides *how* the sign is to be given, in accord with tradition and local culture. In the United States the Bishops' Conference leaves the development of special modes of making the sign to local usage, and neither a specific form nor specific words are determined. However, the bishops may decide whether the sign of peace should be a handshake or a gesture such as a bow of the body. The latter would seem more appropriate in those cultures where "body contact" is not considered to be polite. In some societies in Asia, for example in Thailand, the beautiful joining and raising of hands with an inclination of the head is an ideal gesture for the sign of peace. In some churches in Asia, both sides of the congregation turn to one another and simultaneously make this kind of gesture or a deep bow.

In Western societies, on the other hand, a handshake has various levels of meaning, and there is a risk that the sign of peace might become trivial. The people should be reminded that this is not a time for boisterous conviviality, rather it is a peaceful moment of mutual charity and deep respect for one another as members of the Body of Christ. Children in particular need to be taught the real meaning of the sign, and there seems to be a stage of development when it would be best not to include it in children's Masses, that is, when the children are from about seven to eleven years of age. Experience shows that the sign can degenerate into chaos at this stage unless it is closely supervised. The reasons are obvious: children are not accustomed to shake hands with one another, and bodily contact releases their energies after the peace and recollection of the Eucharistic Prayer.

While respecting local culture, it seems best for the clergy and servers in the sanctuary to retain the gracious Roman custom of a bow and a reverent embrace (not a hug!). The words "Peace be with you" with the response "And also with you" may be used, or some similar formula that is customary (cf. *Ceremonial of Bishops*, no. 103).

7.18 Leaving the Altar for the Sign of Peace

Should the celebrant leave the altar to give the sign of peace to the people? Some priests walk up and down the aisle shaking hands.

Under normal circumstances, no. We are meant to give the sign of peace only to those standing near us, so the celebrant should stay at the altar and give the sign to concelebrants, the deacon and/or servers who are near him or who approach him (cf. *General Instruction of the Roman Missal*, nos. 56 b and 112, *Ceremonial of Bishops*, nos. 99–101, 161). Two practices are thus excluded: (1) the practice in the Missal of St. Pius V of passing it "along the line" from the celebrant through the deacon and subdeacon and so on, and (2) moving about the church and giving the sign to everyone in sight. Servers in the sanctuary and members of the congregation are also not supposed to move around the church giving the sign of peace, because this could imply that they have some privilege or special mandate to go forth greeting everyone.

One exception to this general rule is noted in the *Ceremonial of Bishops*, no. 102. A deacon or concelebrant at a Pontifical Mass goes and gives the sign of peace to the Head of State, when he is officially assisting at Mass. I would add another exception based on common sense. When a priest is celebrating Mass without a server—for example, in the chapel of religious—he may wish to give the sign to someone, so he may choose to leave the altar and go to those nearest him. Nevertheless, it would seem better for someone from the assembly to come to him at the altar to receive the sign of peace from him.

7.19 Deacons or Lay Ministers Breaking the Host?

In some parishes, deacons or even lay ministers of the Eucharist assist at the breaking of Hosts before Communion. Is this correct?

This is not correct. Only the celebrant and concelebrants may break the Hosts at the fraction. This act is seen as pertaining to the sacred fourfold action of the Mass: Our Lord Jesus Christ took bread and wine, He blessed, *He broke*, and then He gave. Therefore the fraction is reserved to bishops and priests. Acting in his very person at the altar, they repeat the sacrificial actions He entrusted to them at the Last Supper. However, according to another ancient tradition, based on practical considerations, deacons and duly authorized extraordinary ministers may assist in the fourth action, the giving of Holy Communion.

This mistaken practice has been proposed as the community "breaking bread", that is, "we all break bread together." While we may figuratively speak in this way, deacons and laity sharing in the fraction is not the Catholic tradition of the East or West. When St. Paul referred to "the bread which we break" (1 Corinthians 10:16), he did not mean that everyone literally broke the Hosts. The sacred priestly role of presiding at the Eucharist was there from the very beginning, inherent in the action of Christ at the Last Supper and his command to the Twelve to "do this". This is evident if one studies the Jewish roots of our faith, the Jewish culture and ritual, in particular the presiding role of the father at the Passover meal and the role of the "elders" of the family of the Church, who made up the council of the priests of the New Covenant. When we start to read trends of our era back into that living tradition, we misrepresent it and end up with abuses, such as this sincerely motivated, but sadly mistaken, fraction rite.

8

DURING AND AFTER
THE COMMUNION RITE

8.1 The Celebrant Receiving the Eucharist Last?

> While travelling in central Europe I noticed in some churches that the celebrant only receives Holy Communion after he has distributed Communion to the faithful. Is this right?

No. This is an example of what happens when one places too much emphasis on the "meal dimension" of the Mass. In fact, it may also indicate a serious misunderstanding of the role of the priest, derived from a preoccupation with the eucharistic meal. Once the Mass is seen first and foremost as a meal, the priest could be regarded as the polite host, who would naturally serve food to his guests first and only eat after they had eaten. But this has never been the practice in the Catholic liturgies of the East or the West precisely because the Mass is first and foremost a sacrifice offered by a priest of the New Testament. It is not a symbolic religious meal hosted by a minister. When offering the Eucharistic Sacrifice, the celebrant first receives the Body and Blood of Christ, which completes the Sacrifice, and then he distributes the Eucharist to the faithful, drawing them into full communion with the Lord's Sacrifice.

The meal dimension of the Mass is always essential, derived from the "communion sacrifices" of the old Israel that Our Lord brought into His action at the Last Supper. The unseen host of this sacred banquet is thus Christ Himself, giving Himself as food and drink for our earthly pilgrimage toward eternal life. The priest, acting in the person of Christ, is also a host, but that is not his primary role.

A priest who has some infectious illness may wish to drink from the chalice after the people. However, to maintain the principles set out above, he should receive first, but by intinction, that is, by dipping the Host into the Blood of Christ, and then he may give Communion to the people.

8.2 Simultaneous Communion

> Should extraordinary ministers and servers receive Communion at the same time as the priest and gathered around the altar?

No. They are not concelebrants. Not even deacons receive the Eucharist simultaneously with the celebrant and concelebrants. Moreover, making a distinction between the Communion of the celebrant and the other ministers and laity is found in all the Rites of the East and West.

This practice raises some historical and doctrinal problems. Some Protestants, from the radical Reformation traditions, practice simultaneous reception of bread and wine. This was introduced deliberately to eliminate distinctions between the ordained sacrificing priest and the faithful and also to express a meal, not a sacrifice. When Catholics introduce simultaneous Communion, it may be done with a good intention, in the name of "participation" or unity. But some of those promoting this practice, like the radical Protestants, also want to blur the difference between the ministerial priesthood and the priesthood of the laity (cf. Vatican II, *Lumen gentium*, no. 10). The mistake we discussed in 7.19, of laity breaking the Hosts at the fraction, seems to be part of the same agenda promoting a "lay-centered church". Inviting everyone to say the words of consecration is perhaps the ultimate error that some extremists have promoted. Once we reach this level, we open the issue currently dividing even the Episcopalians, that is, whether a lay person can preside at the Eucharist. To that proposal the Catholic Church responds with a firm *No*.

8.3 Communion in the Hand

Are there any reasons that would justify refusing to give Holy Communion in the hand?

Pastoral prudence could lead to such a decision, but *only* in a few particular cases. Under normal circumstances, where the options are allowed by the episcopal conference, Communion on the tongue or in the hand are choices that are open to all.

Nevertheless, I know some priests who have refused to give Communion in the hand to children who presented dirty hands to receive Our Lord during a school Mass. The teachers in the parish school soon "got the message" and willingly supervised hand-washing before Mass. They welcomed the priests' stand on such a matter because they perceived the catechetical and spiritual dimension. Parents should also be encouraged to supervise the hand-washing of their own children before receiving the Eucharist at Sunday

Mass. This is how we teach reverence for the Lord Jesus and is a concrete part of preparing to receive him in the Eucharist. Of course it is also normal discipline in the home before meals.

Washing hands before entering church was an ancient custom from the early Christian centuries, which our Islamic brethren seem to have borrowed from us and maintained at their mosques. Our taking holy water at the church door seems to be the last vestige of this early Christian practice.

However, when an adult works in such a way that grime or stains become embedded in the hands that no amount of soap will ever remove, these toil-marked hands can surely welcome Jesus Christ. Some folk in this category become scrupulous about the matter and may need to be told that they still remain free to make their choice on how to receive the Lord.

More delicate cases arise when a frail or very nervous person insists on receiving Communion in the hand but is prone to dropping the Host. A similar case would be a person whose hands are so badly deformed by chronic arthritis that the Host slides off (I have ministered to several people with this problem). In these situations the priest must be very gentle, and we should speak rather of *counsel* than of forbidding an option. The frail person may become discouraged and regard such advice as indicating declining health and fading independence. Nevertheless, in these cases of infirmity, whoever administers the chalice must always keep hold of it and carefully "steer" it to the lips of the communicant, lest the Precious Blood be spilled.

8.4 Children's Communion

Could there be any restrictions on how children receive Communion? Can anyone insist that children only receive on the tongue or in the hand?

Two competent authorities are involved here: (a) the parents, as the primary natural educators and (b) the bishop, as the catechist of the particular Church.

a. I have discussed this problem with various parents, who generally agree that each child should have a choice as to whether he receives on the tongue or on the hand. However, parents may decide that in the case of a certain child, passing through an unsettled or distracted phase, it might be best to insist on receiving directly on the tongue.

b. It seems that the Ordinary could rule that children beneath a certain age are not to receive in the hand. I know of a diocese where this was the rule for some years. I think the policy was well-intentioned, but it led to a strange identification of Communion-in-the-hand as something adults do, hence something one inevitably advances toward, rather than an option. Of course, a priest is not free to make such a ruling.

The second question obviously arises when teachers, catechists or clergy try to make one method of Communion compulsory, usually starting with First Communion training. However, where the options are available, no one can force the little ones into either practice. Thus the training on how to receive Communion should be even-handed, without any bias. In this situation, those outside the child's family also need to be sensitive to family decisions and problems, remembering that the parents are the first educators.

This question raises the need for more careful training in

how to receive the Eucharist reverently and well. Of course such training must be based on precise and clear teaching on transubstantiation and the abiding Real Presence of Our Lord in the sacrament of his love for us. This eucharistic catechesis calls for training in prayer, especially preparation and thanksgiving for the sublime Gift.

8.5 Techniques of Giving Communion

I disagree with your contention in *Ceremonies of the Modern Roman Rite*, no. 337, note 86, that, when Communion is given in the hand, the communicant should step to one side and only then receive the Host. If the communicant receives the Host at once in front of me, I know it has been consumed. Otherwise, when the communicant steps to one side, I cannot see what is happening, and theft of the Eucharist is made easier.

I take your point. This is perhaps a case where both of us are looking for the same results but with different techniques. I can still see "out of the corner of the eye", and I usually note whether the Host has been consumed or not. Once I had to stop distributing Communion and follow a man down the church and ask him whether he really wanted to consume the Host he still held in his hand. He turned out to be merely a rather absent-minded fellow! I think all priests can recount similar unfortunate incidents in this regard. These events call us not only to vigilance but to systematic preaching and teaching on reverence for the Blessed Eucharist.

8.6 Who Can Distribute the Eucharist?

Can altar servers or extraordinary ministers of the Eucharist open the tabernacle and take out the Blessed Sacrament for Communion during Mass?

This question really presupposes the more basic question: Who can distribute Holy Communion during Mass? The only persons who may open the tabernacle during Mass are those authorized to distribute Communion: (1) by virtue of their Sacred Orders, a deacon, priest or bishop; (2) an instituted acolyte who is an extraordinary minister of the Eucharist; (3) an authorized extraordinary minister of the Eucharist. Therefore altar servers are not permitted to open the tabernacle for any purpose, let alone to distribute Communion. An exception could be envisaged in the case of an adult server who was also an authorized extraordinary minister of the Eucharist. But these two ministerial roles are not meant to be combined during the celebration of the Eucharist. With the exception of the instituted acolyte, who approximates the subdeacon in the preconciliar rite, those who serve at the altar should not distribute Communion.

It should also be noted that only *adults* should act as extraordinary ministers of the Eucharist. To choose Catholic schoolchildren to distribute Communion to celebrate their "graduation", for example, is an absurdity based on sentimentality, and sentimentality has inspired liturgical abuses over many centuries. Even in a Catholic high school, it would seem best to reserve this auxiliary ministry to authorized members of the teaching staff, who must be trained carefully beforehand.

8.7 Genuflecting before Communion

I see some people genuflecting before they receive Communion. Is this the right practice?

At present, this reverence before Communion cannot be insisted upon, but it is a good practice because some sign of reverence is "strongly recommended" (*Eucharisticum mysterium*, no. 4; *Inaestimabile donum*, no. 1, citing the *General Instruction of the Roman Missal*, nos. 244 c, 246 b and 247 b). But it is to be made in such a way that it does not disrupt the procession of those going to receive Holy Communion. Those who choose to do this should make the reverence as soon as they are behind the person who is about to receive Communion. This will avoid a possible collision with another communicant or making the priest wait while they genuflect. Because they are aware of these possibilities, some people bow reverently rather than genuflecting. Anyone with a physical problem, or someone who needs to hold onto the end of a pew while genuflecting, could make such a reverence.

8.8 The Communion Plate

I was surprised to see a Communion plate used in a church recently. I thought this had gone out. Is there any provision for this plate in the liturgy today?

Yes. According to the *General Instruction of the Roman Missal*, nos. 246 b and 247 b, the Communion plate is to be held under the chin by the communicant when Holy Communion is given by way of intinction (dipping the Host in the

Blood of Christ). Any drops of the Precious Blood that happen to fall from the Host can be easily caught on the plate. In practice, a server usually holds the plate under the chin of each communicant. Where Communion is administered by intinction, and a plate is not available, a purifier could take its place.

According to the *General Instruction of the Roman Missal*, no. 80 c, and the *Ceremonial of Bishops* no. 125, the plate is to be set out before any celebration of Mass. But as its use is only described in the context of intinction, this may be interpreted to mean that this plate can be *required* only when intinction is to be used at a particular Mass. Nevertheless, it is still customary to use it at all Masses in some churches, especially where the option of kneeling for Communion has been retained. Thus the general use of the Communion plate cannot be forbidden. It remains a licit option, but it is not obligatory.

8.9 Sitting after Communion

> I do not like the present practice of the celebrant and servers sitting for a period of thanksgiving after Holy Communion instead of kneeling, which was the custom before. But some priests say this posture of sitting is obligatory, at least for those in the sanctuary. Is this true?

The *General Instruction of the Roman Missal*, no. 56 j proposes the option of silent prayer after Communion. In that time of silence all "praise God in silent prayer" (*General Instruction*, no. 23). In the Rite of Mass, the rubric says that the celebrant "may return to the chair" for this time of silent prayer. The *Ceremonial of Bishops*, no. 166, says that "all are seated" at this time. Therefore, the celebrant, deacon, concelebrants and servers sit while offering their own silent prayer after Communion. While this applies to all in the sanctuary, I do not think this need be interpreted as strictly obliging all the faithful present at Mass to sit.

This rule applies only to a specified time of personal prayer *after* Communion. During the Communion of the faithful, the celebrant could insist that servers and anyone else in the sanctuary should kneel or stand at their places out of respect for the Blessed Eucharist. In some places, even concelebrants who are not distributing the Eucharist remain standing at their seats until the purification of the vessels begins. Those in the sanctuary should sit only when the celebrant sits. After silent prayer (and/or a thanksgiving hymn or music), he stands and the book bearer attends him at the chair for the Prayer after Communion.

However, the celebrant may choose to say the Prayer after Communion and give the blessing and dismissal at the altar. In this case he may prefer to remain at the altar, standing for the time of silent prayer after Communion, rather than walking to the chair and then back again to the altar. Servers should kneel or stand while the celebrant remains praying silently at the altar.

There would be ground for scandal if anyone were to attempt to force all the faithful to sit *immediately* after Communion. The people remain free to kneel or sit or stand after receiving Holy Communion. Surely the pastoral goal is to encourage personal prayer of thanksgiving. A prudent pastor may justly encourage his people to kneel during and after the time of Communion, even as he should respect their right to choose to sit when he goes to the chair for his own thanksgiving. You should also respect that right.

8.10 Purification of Vessels

> I notice that when some priests purify the paten during
> Mass, they use the purificator instead of the thumb. What
> is the correct requirement?

The purificator or purifier is to be used to purify the paten
during Mass. This is set out in the section of the *General
Instruction of the Roman Missal* on "Purifications", no. 238:
"The paten is usually to be wiped with the purificator." The
reason for this is the favored use of a large paten, which cannot be adequately purified simply by using one's thumb or
fingers, especially when fragments from the broken Host
and people's Hosts accumulate on it. It is to be noted that
the celebrant always breaks the large Host(s) over the paten,
not over the chalice.

Nevertheless, an efficient and reverent technique can
serve as a guide to the celebrant, concelebrants, deacons
and instituted acolytes, who are the only people who purify
the paten(s) and ciboria. The practice, sometimes seen, of
rubbing the paten with the purificator in a circular motion
shows scant respect for the eucharistic fragments, which will
obviously adhere to the purificator. It is better (a) to fold the
purifier over one's fingers and, holding the paten upright in
one's left hand over the chalice or ciborium, (b) to brush
fragments into this vessel, but only with downward strokes.
The celebrant may then tap the folded purifier on the edge
of the vessel to dislodge any fragments that may have ad-
hered to the linen. Water is then used to purify the chalice or
ciborium, and the ablution is immediately consumed from
the chalice. If fragments tend to adhere to a large paten or
ciborium, water may be used to dislodge them, but efficient
"dry" purification is "ordinarily" to be preferred. *General*

Instruction of the Roman Missal, no. 238, still allows for the use of wine and water for the purifications.

I would add the opinion that the purifications are best carried out at the credence table and not at the freestanding altar, where they distract the people after Communion during Mass celebrated "facing the people". It should also be noted that purificators should never be made of synthetic nonabsorbent fabric. Fine linen is always to be preferred on practical grounds, because it absorbs liquid, as well as because of the quality of the fabric.

8.11 Who Can Purify Sacred Vessels?

Are servers or extraordinary ministers permitted to purify the sacred vessels?

Those who purify the sacred vessels after Communion are: (1) a deacon, or, lacking a deacon, a priest concelebrant or celebrant, or, lacking all these, a bishop celebrant; (2) an instituted acolyte, whenever he assists at the altar. Therefore, servers or extraordinary ministers of the Eucharist are not authorized to purify the vessels after Communion. Extraordinary ministers may help consume what remains of the Precious Blood, when Holy Communion has been given under both Species, but they should leave the chalices at the credence table where the deacon(s) and/or instituted acolyte(s) or the celebrant attend to the purifications, which may be deferred until after Mass if this would be more convenient. The extraordinary ministers should purify their fingers in a bowl of water before they return to their places.

8.12 Purifying the Fingers?

> When I went to buy an ablution cup to place near the
> tabernacle, I was told in the church-goods store that they
> no longer sell such objects because the latest law does not
> require the purification of fingers. Is this true?

This is not true. What has changed is that there are now
two ways of purifying one's fingers after handling the Blessed
Sacrament.

1. Since 1967 there has been no obligation for the celebrant to conjoin his fingers from the Consecration of the
Host until after the ablutions. However, the celebrant may
gently move his thumbs and forefingers together, if he needs
to cleanse them of adhering fragments. He does this over
the paten or ciborium, not over the chalice (cf. *General Instruction of the Roman Missal*, no. 237).

2. The option of the purification of fingers with water,
"if necessary", is clearly provided for in the *General Instruction of the Roman Missal*, no. 237. Moreover, according to
the *Ceremonial of Bishops*, no. 166, after Communion, the
bishop's hands are to be washed "if need be". This provision would logically extend to any celebrant or principal
celebrant of a Mass, when others carry out the purification
of the sacred vessels.

Therefore, I would argue that, to provide both options,
all who have distributed Holy Communion, including extraordinary ministers, should have access to an ablution cup
or bowl of water, with a purifier, to wash and dry their
hands. This vessel may be available near the tabernacle or
on a credence table. A person who has distributed Communion where these provisions have not been made should fall
back on procedure (1), that is, carefully rubbing the forefin-

gers and thumbs together over the paten or ciborium before reposing it in the tabernacle or replacing it on the altar.

"Ablution cups" are available in the shops in Rome. But a practical point needs to be noted. The sacristan should be trained to replace the water regularly with pure fresh water, pouring the old water into the sacrarium, the special sacristy sink that leads directly to the earth. He or she should also ensure that the purifier is regularly replaced.

8.13 The Sacrarium

> I was also told in this shop that the sacrarium was no longer required.

The sacrarium, or piscina, is a small sink that leads directly to the earth rather than to the common drains. It is explicitly mentioned in the *General Instruction of the Roman Missal*, no. 239; therefore, every sacristy must be equipped with one. If a sacrarium is not available, water used for purifications should be poured into the font, assuming it has this kind of sink, or directly onto clean earth in a garden or other suitable place.

This all goes to show that we should be careful about opinions proffered in church-goods shops and even what is offered for sale on the basis of such opinions. For example, for their own commercial reasons, some shops sell vestments in forms and colors never envisaged by our Roman Rite, as well as eucharistic vessels that are secular, cheap and break- able, and even, in the U.S., foul-smelling "incense" made of scented wood chips. *Caveat emptor!*

8.14 Reverence for the Blood of Christ

> Recently, while "on supply" in a certain parish, I saw a
> eucharistic minister pour the contents of a chalice down
> the sink after Mass. I protested, but she did not seem to
> understand what I was saying. In fact she said that this
> was what they usually did at that church.

Unfortunately, stories of this kind of profanation of the
Blood of Christ are not uncommon in some countries. The
situation may arise when Communion under both Species
has been given to the faithful or many clergy have concelebrated and much of the Precious Blood remains in chalices.
These are then transferred to the sacristy to be purified after
Mass, and inevitably this task is left to others.

The immediate cause of this grave abuse is removing chalices containing the Precious Blood from the sanctuary and
taking them to a sacristy. This is nowhere envisaged in the
General Instruction of the Roman Missal or the *Ceremonial of
Bishops*. After Communion, chalices containing the Blood of
Christ should be taken to a credence table. Here a priest,
deacon or instituted acolyte purifies these vessels, first consuming the contents of the chalices. He does this after Communion or immediately after Mass. For obvious reasons he
may invite others to consume the Blood of Christ reverently
if much remains.

Certainly the purifications may be deferred until after
Mass, if this is necessary. In this case, the chalices are to
be covered with a veil. However, an extraordinary minister
of the Eucharist or a sacristan is not authorized to purify
chalices or patens. Later these persons may wash the vessels
in the sacristy if they need further cleaning and polishing.
But that cleaning is distinct from the obligatory liturgical

purifications. As I have said elsewhere, in my own opinion, it is always preferable to carry out the purifications at the credence table immediately after Communion and not to defer them until after Mass, when problems like the one you describe can easily arise.

However, in this case we must go to the deeper cause, and that is the fact that the extraordinary minister in question had no awareness of the effect of transubstantiation and the abiding Real Presence of Our Lord under the appearances of wine. This goes to show that diocesan or parish programs for training extraordinary ministers, servers, sacristans, and so on, must include very precise teaching on these truths, with practical applications and relevant rules. However, here we also touch on the void caused by years of inadequate sacramental catechesis in certain countries. There is an urgent need to teach the truths of the Eucharist to all the faithful and to provide precise instruction on reverence for the Blessed Sacrament.

8.15 *The Blood of Christ in the Sacrarium*

> In the case I raised, could the contents of the chalices be poured down the sacrarium? Alternatively, could you reserve the chalices in the tabernacle and use them for Communion at a subsequent Mass?

While it could be argued that pouring the Blood of Christ down the sacrarium is more reverent than using a common drain, it is not permitted to dispose of the contents of the chalice in this way. The remaining Blood of Christ is to be consumed, just as any Hosts in the tabernacle are destined to be consumed.

As to your second suggestion, this practice is not permitted. There is one pastoral exception in the context of ministry to the sick and dying. A small quantity of the Precious Blood may be reserved only to give Communion in the particular case of a sick or elderly person who cannot swallow solid food (cf. *Ceremonies of the Modern Roman Rite*, nos. 625, 626).

9

CONCELEBRATION

9.1 A Concelebrant Reads the Gospel

I have been arguing with some other priests over whether
a concelebrant who is about to read the Gospel should go
to the principal celebrant for his blessing. I claim that this
is only correct when the principal celebrant is a bishop.

You are right. The *Ceremonial of Bishops*, no. 173, has clari-
fied this issue:

1. If the principal celebrant of a concelebrated Mass is
a bishop *and there is no deacon*, the concelebrant who reads
the Gospel first goes to the bishop to receive his blessing.
In a low voice he asks for the blessing, saying, "Your blessing. . . ." He bows profoundly while he is blessed by the
bishop, who makes the sign of the cross over him at the
end of the blessing as he makes the sign on himself. He
stands erect, bows to the bishop and goes to the altar. He
takes the Book of the Gospels from the altar and goes to
the ambo, preceded usually by the thurifer and candle bearers. (If the concelebrant reads the Gospel from a lectionary
already placed on the ambo, he goes directly to the ambo
after receiving the bishop's blessing.)

Having read the Gospel, he sings or says "(This is) the
Gospel of the Lord" and then either takes the open book to

the bishop, who kisses it, or he kisses it himself at the ambo. The traditional practice of taking the Book of the Gospels to the bishop always seems preferable, as it expresses his *episkopé*.

2. If the principal celebrant of a concelebrated Mass is a priest *and there is no deacon*, the concelebrant who reads the Gospel does not go to the principal celebrant to be blessed. Rather, he stands before the altar, where, bowing profoundly, he quietly says "Almighty God, cleanse my heart. . . ." He then goes to the altar and takes the Book of the Gospels and goes to the ambo, preceded usually by the thurifer and candle bearers. (If the concelebrant reads the Gospel from a lectionary already placed on the ambo, he goes directly to the ambo after saying "Almighty God, cleanse my heart. . . .")

Having read the Gospel, he sings or says "(This is) the word of the Lord", and he kisses the open book. He would only need to take the Book of the Gospels or lectionary to the celebrant if the celebrant had indicated that he wanted to preach from the chair, relying on texts in the book.

9.2 *"At Your Hands"?*

It does not seem logical for concelebrants to respond to "Pray brethren . . ." by saying "may the Lord accept the sacrifice at your hands." After all, they are concelebrants and should say "at our hands".

There has never been any directive in this regard. Your proposal could find some support by arguing from the old practice when a priest was celebrating alone and said "at my hands". On the other hand, I would hold that the concelebrants should say "at your hands" when responding to the principal celebrant, because he is the one who presides over the whole eucharistic celebration, and so he takes the bread and wine into his hands at the Consecration. In some places, the people have been told to say "at our hands". There is no authority for this change, which deliberately eliminates the distinct sacrificial action of the celebrant. Unfortunately there are other unsatisfactory proposals to "re-translate" the "Orate fratres" and its response.

9.3 Arranging Concelebrants

I see all sorts of variations in how concelebrants are arranged around the altar at concelebrated Mass. Is there a correct procedure?

Not really. We only have two specific points to guide us: "At the end of the preparation of the gifts, the concelebrants come near the altar and stand around it in such a way that they do not interfere with the actions of the rite and that the people have a clear view. They should not be in the deacon's way when he has to go to the altar in the performance of his ministry" (*General Instruction of the Roman Missal*, no. 167). But we also need to be guided by the sound principles of ecclesial and liturgical hierarchy and a sense of what is noble, simple and fitting. These principles suggest the following preferable arrangement of concelebrants.

Normally, no more than two concelebrants should stand at the altar with the principal celebrant. They need not stand very close to him, nor, as the *General Instruction* indicates, should they ever impede the deacon. They would read aloud those parts of the Eucharistic Prayer that *may* be assigned to the first and second concelebrant. Other concelebrants should be grouped some distance away, preferably arranged in a semi-circle or on each side of the altar, but never as a "block" of clergy looking directly at the people. In fact, it seems best from the aesthetic point of view that only the principal celebrant should stand at the altar, with the deacon standing behind him to his right and all the concelebrants arranged neatly at some distance but still visually "around" the altar. Of course much of this depends on the plan of the sanctuary or the space available.

When the Liturgy of the Eucharist is concelebrated at an altar that is not designed for Mass "facing the people", the concelebrants may best be arranged in parallel lines on each side of the altar or sanctuary, that is, facing across the sanctuary. Thus the faithful have a direct view of the sacred action at the altar in accord with the *General Instruction*, no. 167. This seems to have been the practice at concelebration according to the Rite of Lyons.

9.4 The Silent Concelebrant

> I was concelebrating recently and noticed that the priest next to me said nothing at all at the Consecration. Are concelebrants supposed to pronounce the words of consecration?

Yes, concelebrants must pronounce the words of consecration. When we turn to the *General Instruction of the Roman Missal*, we find that the words are to be *said* (no. 174), but they are to be "recited . . . in a softer voice" (no. 170). This second directive has two purposes: (1) so that the voice of the principal celebrant "stands out clearly. . . . The congregation should be able to hear the text without difficulty"; and (2) by inference, to avoid not only the incoherence of a chorus of male voices reciting a text but also ugliness. The words of consecration may be sung at a solemn eucharistic celebration.

The background to this directive is interesting—and authoritative. On September 22, 1956, in an address to the International Congress on Pastoral Liturgy at Assisi, Pope Pius XII said that concelebrants must say the words of consecration. The Russian practice in the Byzantine Rite would thus be followed when concelebration was properly restored in the Roman Rite, that is, the concelebrants must articulate the words of the epiklesis and the Consecration together with the principal celebrant.

On March 8, 1957, the Holy Office (Congregation for the Doctrine of the Faith) responded to a formal question, or *dubium*, whether concelebrating in silence was valid. The reply was: "Negative, because it is by the institution of Christ that he alone celebrates who pronounces the words of consecration." This response was confirmed by Pope Pius XII, who ordered it to be published. So merely standing in the sanctuary and intending to concelebrate does not suffice. In fact, it is not a valid concelebration of Mass. Moreover, this behavior does not suffice for validity when a priest celebrates Mass privately or when a priest celebrates according to the Missal of St. Pius V—which in fact never envisaged a literally "silent Consecration", as we see from the rubrics and not forgetting that this was the rite in force in 1957 when the decision of the Holy Office was published.

Note, however, that this decision was made six years before the Constitution on the Liturgy of the Second Vatican Council, *Sacrosanctum concilium*, no. 57, which restored the full use of concelebration to the Roman Rite. This fact breaks down irresponsible criticisms of concelebration made by some "traditionalists".

One wonders why a concelebrant would stand mute at the Consecration. There are some possible explanations. When we insist too much on the concelebrants saying the words quietly, some priests may react by saying nothing and "mentally" consecrating. But most concelebrants conform to the normal practice of quietly articulating the words. On the other hand, other priests may be following a liturgist's theory, influenced by oriental practice and speculation about what may have happened in the early Church, that "concelebration" simply means priests being present at the altar. But in the modern Roman Rite concelebrating is a visible sacramental sign, not only in presence and deed, but in word.

9.5 *The Doxology at a Concelebrated Mass*

> During a concelebrated Mass, patens, ciboria and chalices were passed along the altar so that each concelebrant had something to raise at the final doxology of the Eucharistic Prayer. This is quite common in our country. Is it correct?

No. This is a fussy practice. It is not fitting, even if it seems to arise from a sincere desire to "involve" all the concelebrants and "give them something to do". At the final doxology of the Eucharistic Prayer, there are only three options at concelebrations: (1) the principal celebrant raises the paten, and the deacon raises the chalice; (2) when there is no deacon, the principal celebrant raises both himself; or (3) he raises the paten, and the first concelebrant raises the chalice. I note that the vessels were passed "along the altar", which indicates that everyone was crowded around it—another reason for this kind of fussiness.

9.6 Communion of Concelebrants

Should concelebrants be receiving Communion during or after the laity receive Communion?

The *General Instruction of the Roman Missal*, no. 201, (a) allows the principal celebrant, after his own Communion, to proceed with giving Communion to the faithful while the concelebrants drink from the Chalice. A small number of concelebrants could, and surely should, receive *both* the Body and Blood of the Lord before the faithful, but waiting for a large number of concelebrants to finish receiving the Eucharist would delay the Communion of the faithful. Nevertheless, a practical and serious problem could arise if the chalices were found not to contain enough of the Precious Blood for the concelebrants because the laity had already received under both kinds. In these situations, care needs to be taken to ensure that there are enough chalices set aside on the altar for concelebrants.

9.7 Reaction against Concelebration

In recent years, especially in North America, there has been a reaction against concelebration in some circles. How do you explain this?

I discovered this phenomenon while representing the Vatican at a seminar held at a major Catholic university. On

going to the sacristy I found myself to be the only concelebrant accompanying a slightly embarrassed bishop. I concelebrated and read the Gospel, but the other clergy present
did not concelebrate and chose to remain among the religious and lay participants. I later learned that this is spine-
less male conformism to a feminist decree: priests must not
"offend women" by the exclusive sign of an all-male team
looking at them from the altar! Apparently I was forgiven
for my politically incorrect behavior, probably because "he
is from Rome", an Australian who "does not know any better"! Such is the way we drift when the virus of ideology
penetrates Christian worship.

On the other hand, some traditionally minded people re-
ject concelebration because they see it as undermining the
right of priests to celebrate their daily Mass privately, that is,
without a congregation. In fact no one can oblige a priest to
concelebrate, just as no one can oblige a priest to celebrate
alone. The options should remain open, especially in communities of clergy, and this seems to be the general trend
today in monasteries, religious houses, seminaries, clergy
houses, and so on. But a priest who resolutely refuses ever
to concelebrate has not really assimilated the meaning of
the "presbyterium", especially when Mass is concelebrated
with the diocesan bishop. All priests should at least concelebrate on Holy Thursday, when we recall the sublime gift
of the ministerial priesthood that Our Lord imparted at the
Last Supper.

10

LITURGICAL AND
SACRAMENTAL PROBLEMS

10.1 Accidents, Mistakes and Incidents

In times past ordinands had to study *De Defectibus* at the front of the Roman Missal, an instruction covering all sorts of accidents and mistakes that could even invalidate the Mass. I find no such treatise in the modern Roman Missal. Where can I find such guidance today, and has anything changed in this regard?

The instruction *De Defectibus in Celebratione Missae Occurentibus* covered problems that can arise. The ten short chapters extended over four areas: (1) defects in the matter of the Eucharist; (2) defects in the form used for consecrating the Eucharist; (3) defects in the celebrant himself; (4) problems caused by accidents or incidents that may occur during Mass. Today the essential positions taken in the four areas in *De Defectibus* can be found distributed among various official postconciliar sources that include liturgical laws. However, these positions are now expressed in a positive sense, to exclude defects by saying what ought to be done rather than by beginning with the problems. I will follow the structure of *De Defectibus* and indicate the current sources.

1. *Defects in the matter of the Eucharist:* Only wheaten bread must be used, and it is to be recently baked to avoid cor-

ruption (cf. Canon 924 §2). Only natural grape wine is to be used, and it must be uncorrupt (cf. Canon 924 §3). The bread in the Roman Rite is to be unleavened (cf. Canon 926). The wine is to be natural and not mixed with any foreign substance; the bread and wine are to be in a good condition (cf. *General Instruction of the Roman Missal*, nos. 284, 285).

2. *Defects in the form used for consecrating the Eucharist:* The words of consecration were defined by Pope Paul VI, Apostolic Constitution *Missale Romanum*, April 3, 1969 (printed at the front of the altar edition of the missal). It is assumed that the celebrant will use these words in their integrity and that they will be said clearly and audibly, cf. *General Instruction of the Roman Missal*, nos. 12 and 170, and the rubric before the Consecration in the *Order of Mass*.

3. *Defects in the celebrant himself:* These were covered under three headings: the intention of the celebrant, the disposition of his soul, the disposition of his body.

a. *The celebrant's intention:* Nothing is clearly stated in current official sources about the intention, but the general principle of "intending to do what the Church intends" still applies. Moreover, the celebrant will at least have a virtual intention now that the Eucharistic Prayer and the words of consecration are pronounced aloud. However, I believe we would need to go beyond the principle assumed in *De Defectibus* of only intending to consecrate what is placed on the corporal. This should be widened to intending to consecrate whatever is brought to the altar to be consecrated. This would cover various situations when all the vessels are not placed on the corporal and thus eliminate scruples.

b. *The celebrant's spiritual disposition:* A priest in a state of grave sin is not to celebrate Mass before making sacramental confession, or before making an act of contrition when he is obliged to offer Mass and it is not possible for him to go to confession first (cf. Canon 916).

c. *The celebrant's physical disposition:* The priest is to be fasting for at least one hour before receiving the Eucharist (cf. Canon 919 §1). But if he binates or trinates, he may eat or drink something before the second or third celebration, even if there is not an hour's interval (cf. Canon 919 §2). There is no binding fast for clergy who are elderly or ill (cf. Canon 919 §3).

4. *Problems caused by accidents or incidents during Mass:* Matters covered in the first part of chapter 10 in *De Defectibus* should now be interpreted in the light of Canon 932, on the sacred place and the altar, and Canon 929, on the vestments. The requirements for the altar and for the celebration of Mass are set out in the *General Instruction of the Roman Missal,* nos. 259–70, 281–312. There are now very few restrictions on the time when Mass can be celebrated (cf. Canon 931). If the Host falls, it is to be picked up reverently; if the Precious Blood is spilled, the area should be washed and the water is then to be poured into the sacrarium (cf. *General Instruction of the Roman Missal,* no. 239). When the celebrant finds he has "consecrated" water rather than wine, he replaces the water with wine and water and consecrates the contents of the chalice without consecrating the bread again (cf. *General Instruction of the Roman Missal,* no. 286). These matters and some other questions are presented in *Ceremonies of the Modern Roman Rite,* appendix 6, "Accidents".

From these sources, it can be seen that nothing significant has changed with regard to most of *De Defectibus,* so it would still be useful to read it. However, taking into account the problems that continue to arise, even if in the context of modified legislation and new rubrics, it is to be hoped that some new form of this instruction might be published by the competent authority. It would benefit the clergy and especially candidates preparing for ordination. In these times, I do not believe it would encourage scruples. We all like to know where we stand.

10.2 Unforeseen Problems at Mass

I go to several distant mission stations to celebrate Mass. At times basic problems arise. For example, in one place another priest had taken the sacred vessels away with him. Then there was the time when I found the bread and wine unfit to use, because of the tropical climate. In another church, after a downpour that drenched the sacristy, I found that the missal was ruined and I could not even turn the pages. What does one do in such situations, when one does not want to deprive people of the Mass?

In these situations all we can do is our best. But "our best" includes making prudent judgments about what elements are so essential that their absence would justify *not* celebrating Mass for the people in an unforeseen situation. Let us take each of the situations you raise and make some distinctions.

1. *There is no chalice and paten at the church, and it would take much time to procure these vessels from elsewhere.* In this situation, you could use decent secular vessels to celebrate Mass, since what was lacking was not essential for the confection of the Eucharist. The problem must be explained to the people to avoid scandal. I would add that a glass and plate so used should then be set aside and later destroyed and buried, with compensation offered to whoever provided them. The same logic applies to a lack of vest-

ments, although the priest normally brings at least an alb with him.

2. *The bread and wine are in a very poor condition.* Here we are faced with a serious problem, because *no one is free to use doubtful matter for the Eucharist.* A further problem (and this has happened) would be nausea or even a danger to health involved in using moldy bread or corrupt wine, both of which are rejected in Canon 924 §2 and §3. The easy way out of such a dilemma would be to seek some ordinary leavened wheaten bread and grape wine from among the people. But let us suppose that the priest is working in a culture where only bread made from rice or corn and fruit wine or liquor are available. He cannot use such invalid matter for the Eucharist, as we see from Canon 924. Therefore it would not be possible to celebrate Mass on that occasion. But the people would merit a sensitive explanation, followed by a non-eucharistic act of worship and the promise of a visit in the near future when the priest would celebrate Mass for them.

3. *The missal cannot be used, and a people's missal is not available to take its place.* If the celebrant is confident that he can remember the essential prayers of the Mass, he surely would be free to put the rite together from memory, even if it has to be in a language that the people did not understand, as could happen were an English or French-speaking missionary to find himself with no access to texts in the local language. Those with memory problems, with scruples or a fear of "going blank" would do best to sit down before the Mass and write out the main prayers as best they could recall them, even if this involved simplifying the text. Here every effort should be made not to deny the people the Mass because of the lack of a nonessential.

However, there is a general solution to all these problems.

When a priest can never be quite sure what awaits him in the sacristy of a distant church, he should always bring a Mass kit with bread and wine in secure containers, a chalice and paten, a missal and the eucharistic vestments. Even if he usually finds everything in order, he should nonetheless ensure that nothing is lacking for the worthy celebration of the Eucharistic Sacrifice, for he has been ordained as a "steward of the mysteries".

10.3 Liturgical Law in Difficult Situations

We have all heard stories of Mass celebrated in a secret way in times of persecution, especially under Communism. Mass was offered in a disguised form in restaurants, private homes or prison camps, but all the ceremonial adjuncts were set aside. What is your view of these events, that is, in the light of liturgical law? Can these practices be a precedent that justifies adapting in other situations?

Again we have to make the distinction between essentials and nonessentials. However, here we are not dealing with unforeseen circumstances, rather with a situation of grave emergency, when the very lives of the faithful were under threat. The liturgical laws governing what is not essential to the *valid* celebration of Mass and the sacraments only bind under normal circumstances, that is, when it is reasonably *possible* to observe them. Threat of death could mean it was not reasonably possible to observe the cultus of the Church, and a priest could make a prudent judgment to set certain signs and symbols aside to protect others. Competent ecclesiastical authorities usually make these possibilities clear to their clergy who are forced to work under such dangerous conditions.

Nevertheless, the liturgical and sacramental essentials, such as valid matter and form, the required minister and intention, must never be set aside. In practice, under the most difficult conditions, priests and laity have heroically observed these essentials. Some of them recount how they discovered a deeper faith in the Mass and the sacraments through concentrating on the essentials.

However, I would add that, at times, persecuted Christians have not readily set aside all the nonessential signs and symbols. For example, although the Nazis permitted the many priests in Dachau to set up a dignified chapel, where Mass was celebrated, they would not think of allowing anyone to be ordained there. So, for the ordination of Bl. Karl Leisner, all the requirements were smuggled in, so that Bishop Piguet of Clermont-Ferrand was able to ordain him early in the morning of December 17, 1944, with the full rite of the Church. As it turned out there was a sweet providence in all this. Fr. Leisner was only able to offer one precious Mass before he succumbed to tuberculosis, but he who would later be raised to our altars was ordained under circumstances of dignity and honor. I also think of the English martyrs of the Reformation era, who took great pains to celebrate Mass correctly, even under the most dangerous and difficult circumstances. They became particularly ingenious in concealing the vessels and vestments, which they valued as part of their Catholic identity and heritage.

Yet, under the closer gaze of Communist tyrants, even these precautions were not enough. I know a young Slovakian priest who was ordained in five minutes with the television blaring in the room. As an "underground priest", he often celebrated Mass in his room using a wine glass and plate. We are not talking of the 1950s but of the late 1980s, just before the "velvet revolution" freed his suffering people. Today he staunchly maintains the liturgical norms of the Church. He knows how these norms also represent religious freedom—the liberty to worship God in public, the liberty of liturgy.

As to your second question, I know that some try to justify their own refusal to observe liturgical law by appealing to what was done in a prison camp, or to a Mass celebrated in Graham Greene's novel about the persecution in Mexico, or they cite the precautions of my Slovakian friend. This kind of emotive argument has no logical basis, because we enjoy the freedom to observe the liturgical laws of the Church. It also seems to be an implicit insult to the memory of our martyrs and heroes, who *reluctantly* set aside the very signs and symbols that those who invoke their example seem to find somewhat inconvenient.

10.4 Desecration of the Holy Eucharist

What should be done when Hosts are found unconsumed, for example, discarded on or under the seats or left between the pages of a hymnbook?

Unfortunately this is a recurring problem. Some persons take the Host in the hand. Rather than consuming it, for their own reasons, they conceal it and discard it in the church or elsewhere. When a discarded Host is found in a clean condition, it should be immediately consumed. If it is soiled or has been stuck beneath the seat with saliva (I know of such cases), it should be immediately placed in a vessel of water that is then kept in a secure place such as the safe for sacred vessels. After some days the contents of this vessel are poured down the sacrarium. From time to time, the pastor may wish to look under the seats in his church to see whether this abuse of the Eucharist has occurred.

However, when these situations arise, the pastor should prudently avoid making a public outcry, and he may need to silence the person who found the Host. But he would be morally bound to take some steps to ensure that this sacrilege does not occur again. He could preach on the need to consume the Host immediately, explaining that no one is obliged to come to Communion. He could remind his people that those who do not approach the altar are not necessarily in a state of sin. He may also ask some parishioners to watch the behavior of persons accustomed to sit in the part of the church where the Host was found. This had to be done in one parish to resolve the more serious case of a youth who was stealing Hosts and selling them to a satanist.

10.5 Confessional Practice after Profanation

What should a confessor do when a penitent confesses that he has discarded the Host?

This is not a liturgical question, but there seems little point in dealing with the profanation of the Eucharist without adding the sacramental and pastoral remedies. Some distinctions should be made here because varying levels of culpability may be discerned, as may be seen from these cases.

1. A person who "throws away" the Host has committed a sin that incurs automatic excommunication (*latae sententiae*). The remission of this penalty is reserved to the Holy

See (cf. Canon 1367). If a penitent confesses that he did this, the confessor should then ask what the motive was for such sacrilege. If the penitent intended to desecrate the Host or to show contempt or rejection of Our Lord, then the matter must go to the Ordinary, so that recourse can be made to the Holy See. Only after an affirmative response from the Holy See can absolution be granted and a significant penance imposed. The penitent must be informed not only of the gravity of the sin but also of the penalty that he has incurred and of the steps that must be taken to lift the excommunication. He will need instruction on what excommunication involves and should be told that this is not a permanent state but that one cannot approach the sacraments until the penalty is lifted. I knew of a case where a devout man imagined that being excommunicated was a permanent state. It was doubtful whether he had incurred the penalty, but this misunderstanding kept him from the sacraments for thirty years.

2. However, a person may have discarded the Host out of fear of making a sacrilegious Communion, for example, a young person feigning to go to Communion to keep up appearances with family or friends. Although the sacrilege occurred, it could be argued that the penitent had acted sacrilegiously to avoid what he regarded as a greater sacrilege, that is, an unworthy Communion. Due to inadequate awareness of the gravity of discarding the Sacred Species, there may not be an intention to "throw away", that is, to desecrate the Eucharist. But because there may be doubt here, particularly in the case of young people over the age of sixteen (cf. Canon 1323, 1), absolution should be deferred while the matter is put to the Ordinary. It would seem prudent, at this stage, not to inform the penitent of a possible state of excommunication, while making it clear that the

matter is very serious, that it requires deferred absolution and a significant penance and that the penitent cannot approach the Eucharist until absolution has been granted.

3. The much rarer case of ignorance may involve confused eucharistic faith due to poor catechesis. A very ignorant person may believe that he is supposed to approach the altar but then need not necessarily consume the Host. Beginning to doubt this behavior, he then raises the matter in confession. In this case, after due questioning, admonition and instruction, the priest can absolve, without any reference to the canonical penalty, which remains undiminished only if the ignorance is "crass, supine or affected" (Canon 1325). If there is doubt about this, the case must be referred to the Ordinary. In all cases of ignorance, the specific penance required by the confessor could relate directly to devotion to the Blessed Sacrament and catechesis on the Real Presence, so as to have a pedagogical dimension. The *latae sententiae* penalty may be diminished, but a penance takes its place (cf. Canon 1324).

4. A drunken person manages to approach Communion and then throws away the Sacred Host and is later penitent for this act. Here the confessor may absolve and impose a significant penance in place of the penalty, because the penalty of excommunication is diminished (cf. Canon 1324 §1, 2). This does not apply, however, when someone has deliberately become intoxicated in order to have the courage to profane the Eucharist (cf. Canon 1325). Then we are in the grave area of case 1.

5. The priest may absolve a penitent who was forced to profane the Eucharist by another party (cf. Canons 1323, 3 and 1324 §1, 5). This may have been the case with the youth who stole Hosts for the satanists. He may have acted out of fear for his life.

6. Mentally confused persons who raise this matter in confession should be treated with great compassion, prudently counseled and absolved, according to the principle included in the qualifying words that were formerly said during absolution, "in quantum possum et tu indiges" (insofar as I am able and you request it). This may be inferred from Canons 1322 and 1323, 6, but these canons are qualified by Canons 1324 §1, 2, and 1325. In some cases, especially when scruples or religious mania are a problem, mentally unstable persons have imagined that they acted in this way.

Another related problem arises when someone keeps the Sacred Host for his own purposes but without desecration. Religious fanatics occasionally do this for their own peculiar devotional purposes. But more often than not this is a case of ignorance today, as with the young non-Catholic bride who had married a Catholic and proudly showed her album of wedding photos to a priest. Here he found a Host, under the plastic page cover. It was a keepsake of the happy day that she had taken in her hand and not consumed. One wonders why she was offered Communion, and at a Nuptial Mass that was clearly inappropriate for this interchurch marriage. In these situations a priest has a duty to do everything reasonably possible to retrieve the Host and consume it or dispose of it in one of the ways indicated in the reply to question 10.4.

These problems underline the need for every Ordinary to forbid a practice that has crept into some parishes, that is, when ushers make the people come to Communion in rows. This assumes that everyone at Mass *must* come to Communion, even a Buddhist student who is a guest in a Catholic family or a divorced and remarried Catholic who is not allowed to receive the Eucharist. Such persons, finding themselves inadvertently in possession of the Host, may be tempted to discard or keep it.

10.6 Mass Celebrated Alone

> When there is no urgency for a Mass (for example, to consecrate holy Viaticum), can a priest who is travelling celebrate Mass all alone, with no server or other person present? His only reason for celebrating is that he values his daily Mass, and sometimes it is not convenient to find a place to celebrate Mass with others present.

The *General Instruction of the Roman Missal*, no. 211, says that a priest may not celebrate Mass without even a server present, "*except for serious necessity*". However, the 1983 Code takes a more moderate pastoral position, in the light of typical modern situations when there is no one around to serve or answer a Mass, for example, in the case of a retired priest who lives alone. Canon 906 says: "A priest may not celebrate [the Eucharistic Sacrifice] without the participation of at least some member of the faithful, except for *a just and reasonable cause*."

To find such "a just and reasonable cause", we turn to Canon 904: "Indeed, daily celebration is strongly recommended, since even if the faithful cannot be present, it is the act of Christ and the Church in which priests fulfill their principal function." What Holy Mother Church earnestly recommends is always "just and reasonable". Therefore, any priest, whether travelling or not, may celebrate Mass on his own, because the "just and reasonable cause" would be exercising his priesthood through the deeply ecclesial practice of daily Mass.

10.7 Mass Celebrated Alone and Silently?

I live in a house with other priests who are pursuing higher studies. I have noted that when some of these priests celebrate Mass alone, they read all the prayers and readings in complete silence, without even moving their lips. Is this permitted?

No. In the light of the reply I gave above about silent concelebrants, we can see that this abuse is covered by the decision of Pope Pius XII and the response of the Holy Office (1956, 1957), which was later embodied in the rubrics of the modern Roman Rite. Some young priests may imagine that silently celebrating Mass is being very "traditional", whereas in fact it is simply liturgically wrong and was never envisaged in the preconciliar liturgy, because the so-called "silent Canon" was said *sotto voce*, not read silently. More seriously, this practice can invalidate the Mass. Of course, a priest celebrating alone may choose to read the prayers and readings in a low voice, even a whisper, but he is not free to read them silently. As already noted, this applies above all to the words of consecration, which must be articulated lest the Mass be rendered invalid.

10.8 An Unusual Case of Mass Celebrated Alone

A priest celebrates Mass on his own in a religious community where there are brethren willing to serve his Mass. When they offer to serve, he sends them away, because, he says, the presence of anyone disturbs him when he likes to meditate during Mass. Should this priest's superiors correct him? Is he acting according to liturgical law?

His superiors should correct him. He is acting against the provision in Canon 906, which does not allow Mass alone "except for *a just and reasonable cause*". As I have already observed, to maintain one's practice of celebrating a daily Mass would be a just and reasonable cause. But to maintain one's spirit of recollection is surely an inadequate cause.

Nevertheless, the correction in this case should take the gentle form of inviting this priest to reflect on the meaning of the celebration of Mass, in the context of the liturgy of the Church. He obviously is a sincere and prayerful priest, but he has turned the Mass into his own private meditation, something that it is not. A priest may and should meditate before and after Mass, and all priests should celebrate Mass prayerfully, in a recollected spirit. But no priest should intrude his own personal devotions into the liturgy or bend the liturgical law of the Church to accommodate such devotions.

10.9 Permission for a "Home Mass"

What permission is required for the celebration of Mass in a private dwelling, that is, a "home Mass"?

There are two steps. First, it should be ascertained whether the Ordinary of the place (the diocesan bishop or his equivalent in law) allows these eucharistic celebrations and under what circumstances they may take place. Once this has been verified, the parish priest or his equivalent in law may give or withhold permission for a "home Mass". No priest should enter a parish to celebrate the Eucharist in a private dwelling without the permission of the pastor. A priest who is a house guest, for example, during a vacation, should not presume this permission, unless the nearest church is very distant or cannot be made available for his Mass.

Masses celebrated in a private dwelling are usually not allowed on Sundays or solemnities, except under unusual or pressing circumstances. On Sundays or solemnities, the cathedral, parish churches and other public churches or chapels are the places where Christ's faithful gather to celebrate His Sacrifice. The Ordinary may also wish to set other liturgical conditions to ensure a worthy celebration of the Eucharist. He may limit "home Masses" to mark specific family occasions or as part of a parish mission or spiritual renewal program or according to the custom of a religious movement or apostolate. He may, and should, permit these Masses to meet the spiritual needs of aged or infirm persons who are unable to leave their houses or apartments.

11

SACRAMENTAL PRACTICE

11.1 Reconciliation of Converts

> I recall in the past that, after conditional Baptism, con
> verts to the faith had to kneel and recite the Tridentine
> Profession of Faith and renounce Protestant error. Now
> I gather all they need do is say the Apostles' Creed. Does
> this not trivialize reception into the Church?

I regret to say that your information is inadequate. The reception of converts has certainly not been trivialized. The
current *Rite for the Reconciliation of Baptized Christians* should
be studied carefully. Certainly, the act of faith is the Apostles' Creed, that is, the baptismal creed, but this is followed
by a declaration by the convert that he accepts *all* that the
Catholic Church teaches and believes.

Because the reconciliation of baptized Christians is seen
in the broader context of the Rite of Christian Initiation of
Adults (RCIA), the celebration of the sacraments now stands
out more prominently. The actual ceremony of reception
normally takes place during a Mass and centers around the
Sacrament of Confirmation, which any priest reconciling a
convert is automatically delegated to administer. Then the
new Catholic receives his First Holy Communion at that
Mass. It is through the ontological effects of the character

sacraments and the Holy Eucharist that we are transformed into living members of the Mystical Body of Christ.

It is assumed that the convert has been instructed thoroughly and understands what he is accepting by being reconciled to the true Church. Thus the renunciation of error is taken for granted, especially in an ecumenical context when we realize that it is not always just to attribute *formal* heresy ("Protestant error" as you put it) and schism to persons raised outside the Catholic Church. I was raised an Anglican, and my father was an Anglican pastor, so I appreciate this from personal experience. In many cases, for example when reconciling Protestant and Anglican clergymen, there is a positive emphasis on the rich elements of faith and sanctification already received outside of visible communion with the Successor of Peter. These divine gifts will be perfected through reconciliation and full communion with the authentic Universal Church.

Nevertheless, the sacramental and penitential discipline is maintained. The convert goes to confession and receives absolution *before* the ceremony of reception. This is clearly to restore the justifying grace of Baptism already received. In cases where there is any doubt about the valid reception of Baptism, a conditional Baptism is administered privately *before* he makes a personal confession. With the regrettable spread of New Age ideas and feminism and modernism within separated ecclesial communions, it would seem prudent for pastors to be attentive to the need for conditional Baptism, even in the case of receiving members of respectable mainstream religious bodies. It is alleged that some clergy in these denominations do not baptize in the name of the Holy Trinity, ecumenical agreements about the matter and form of Baptism notwithstanding.

11.2 *Valid Matter for the Eucharist*

What matter is required for a valid consecration at Mass?
May any type of bread and wine be used?

This question has arisen because of "experiments" or attempts to make the sacramental signs seem more vivid. But
the Code of Canon Law governing the Roman Rite is clear
and simple. Only wheaten bread (cf. Canon 924 §2; *General
Instruction of the Roman Missal*, no. 282) and wine made from
grapes are to be used (cf. Canon 924 §3; *General Instruction
of the Roman Missal*, no. 284). So it is not true that any type
of bread and wine may be used.

In the Mass of the Roman Rite and other Western Rites
and uses, this bread is to be unleavened (Canon 926), "in
accordance with the ancient tradition of the Latin Church",
apparently derived from the unleavened bread of the Passover (cf. 1 Corinthians 5:6–8). The flat round loaves dis-
played on the altar in the beautiful sixth-century mosaic of
Melchisedech in the Church of San Vitale, Ravenna, seem to
be unleavened. In our Latin tradition, the eucharistic bread
is made only of wheat flour and water. It should be properly
baked so as to be neither uncooked or too hard. Wholemeal
flour may be used, and the bread may take a more substantial form than in the past. A larger form of the traditional
round Host may be broken into fragments at the fraction
(cf. *General Instruction of the Roman Missal*, no. 283).

It is illicit to use leavened bread in the Roman Rite instead
of unleavened bread. However, in an emergency, when the
usual eucharistic bread is not available, leavened wheaten
bread may be used for Mass. On the other hand, when we
turn to *some* Eastern Rites, this tradition and the liturgical
law are reversed. Leavened bread is the norm, often baked

by the clergy, and in these Rites the unleavened bread of our Rite could be used only in an emergency.

The problem of valid matter only begins once we move away from simple wheaten bread to recipes for homemade "bread" that is more like a muffin, sweet bun or cake. Recipes for making this kind of eucharistic bread usually date from the sixties and seventies, and may appear from time to time in fringe circles. Some include such ingredients as honey, sugar, shortening, butter or oil, corn flour, chemical colorings and even spice or raisins! *This "bread" is invalid matter for the Eucharist.* Were a small amount of any of these ingredients to be added to wheaten bread, the matter would be doubtful, and *no priest may use doubtful matter to confect the Eucharist.*

Pure grape wine is to be used for the Eucharist. In Europe, and increasingly in North America, light table wine is used. In countries that do not produce wine, and even in some former mission territories that do produce wine, a fortified wine is still preferred, that is, a stronger wine that will keep under hot or humid conditions after the bottle is opened. The percentage of alcohol added to preserve "altar wine" varies from country to country. But heavily fortified wines are not permitted. The Ordinary is to determine what wine may or may not be used in the light of its purity and the alcoholic content. The quality of altar wine officially endorsed in some regions could well be improved. The color is irrelevant, but red or rosé may be regarded as a better eucharistic sign than white wine. On the other hand, white wine is often chosen because it does not stain the altar linens.

In the light of this question, it is best to buy the bread and wine only from authorized church suppliers, especially agencies that provide eucharistic matter carefully prepared by religious communities. Purchasing through these agencies recognizes the devotion of religious men and women and is also a way of assisting them financially. Using bread bought in shops is also problematical in countries where all sorts of flour, and milk, vegetable matter and even chemicals are added to table bread. The trend of using "ethnic bread" also has some pitfalls. While Passover matsos and pita bread may be valid matter, in India they make some bread from lentil flour. Commercial wine, especially the bulk wines sold in plastic casks, raises problems. It may not be pure *grape* wine, and it may contain some foreign substance, forbidden in the *General Instruction of the Roman Missal*, no. 284. Homemade wine is also problematical. In the seminary we were told the cautionary tale of the farmer who always made the altar wine for the village church. One year he came to the priest and said that he could not provide the wine because his apple harvest had been so poor!

In the name of inculturation some have also sought to use corn bread or rice bread and wine made from fruit or even beer at the altar. They argue that this is meaningful matter derived from the diet of the local people. Such proposals reveal an exaggerated notion of inculturation and have never been countenanced by the Holy See.

11.3 Bringing the Eucharist to the Sick

> According to the former Roman Ritual, it was required that when a priest took the Blessed Sacrament to the sick, he was to be accompanied by a lay person. Is this still obligatory?

This is not obligatory. In fact, one lay escort was a concession, because, in a Catholic social context, a team of servers was envisaged, accompanying the priest in procession to the sick person's house, with candles, bell and even a *baldachin* (canopy) or *ombrellino* (liturgical umbrella) held over the Blessed Sacrament. In the modern situation, it is still fitting that the priest, deacon or an extraordinary eucharistic minister be accompanied by another person, if not on the journey to the house or apartment, at least when he arrives there. In some difficult situations it would seem prudent also to have someone always present, to protect the Eucharist from profanation and to ensure the personal security of the eucharistic minister.

But there is a deeper ecclesial justification for someone escorting a eucharistic minister and assisting at these rites. It is a way all baptized Christians can share concretely in "this ministry of mutual charity within the Body of Christ", participation that brings out the community aspect of celebrating the sacraments of the sick (cf. *Roman Ritual, Pastoral Care of the Sick*, general introduction, no. 33). What is also envisaged is not only that members of the family and friends join in the prayers with the sick person but even that they might receive Holy Communion, whenever this is possible on such an occasion. Moreover, the faithful should be trained and catechized in this ministry (cf. ibid., no. 6). I believe this training should begin with children at about the age of ten or eleven, when they are interested in the details of ceremony and religious procedures, which should find a major part in their catechesis.

Therefore, the custom of a lay person preceding the eucharistic minister and carrying a candle or lamp and ringing a small bell has much to commend it in Catholic hospitals and institutions. The nursing staff should be trained to welcome and reverently and silently accompany the clergy or other ministers who bring the Eucharist to the sick or aged in these places. Hospital chaplains should insist on such reverence for Our Lord, and they should strongly protest if hospital staff behave otherwise. In a pluralist society, non-Catholics in the caring professions are usually very respectful of our religion once they are made aware of our practices and customs. Nor let us forget the evangelistic impact of reverent sacramental ministry in a secularized context.

11.4 *A Pill Box Is Not a Pyx*

> In our parish some people take the Eucharist to sick relatives or friends. I know this is permitted, but they use pill boxes instead of pocket pyxes, and one person goes to coffee after Mass and chats before taking Communion to the sick. This does not seem right to me.

Any parish can afford to buy enough suitable pyxes for those who have been delegated to take Communion to the sick. Using a locket or a pill box as a pyx is not worthy of the Eucharist, and this practice, like the use of secular vessels, already noted above in question 2.4, is not permissible.

Anyone authorized to take the Eucharist to the sick must go directly from the church to the place where the sick person lives or is under care. During that journey, it is customary not to speak to anyone, except out of necessity. Prayer and recollection should occupy those who are privileged to carry the Blessed Sacrament during this ministry. Moreover, no one is permitted to leave the Eucharist in his home or car before or after taking God's sublime Gift to the sick.

11.5 *An Unusual Request*

> Can I accede to the request of a person who asks to be
> given two or three Hosts together, even a large Host, so
> that the divine presence within him will last longer? Is
> this lawful?

Here we are not dealing with the law but with common
sense and prudence. The person who makes this unusual
request may be devout and sincere, but bestowing this kind
of favor is only encouraging a possible spiritual imbalance.
I would add the opinion that it is an inadequate theology
that makes our bodies only fleshly tabernacles for the Eucharist, until the Species deteriorates. This is far from what
Our Divine Lord teaches in John 6 about the eucharistic
union with Him and seems not unrelated to the curious devotion to Jesus as a "prisoner" in the Sacred Species or in
the tabernacle.

This devout person should be invited to reflect more
deeply on the abiding union of Jesus Christ with the soul of
each well-disposed communicant. He may be encouraged to
look at the prayer life of the great saints for guidance. They
continued their thanksgiving throughout the day, long after
the Sacred Species had been digested.

In the public worship of the Church, granting special favors to individuals is always fraught with pastoral dangers.
When there is a just cause, some adaptation to individuals
should be made, for example, not offering the chalice to persons who cannot take alcohol or offering only the chalice
to persons unable to tolerate the gluten content of wheaten
bread. But we must avoid any practices that encourage spiritual fantasy among the devout or that might arouse *admi-
ratio* (scandal) among the faithful.

11.6 Marriage Facing the People

> I notice that some priests arrange the bride and groom
> and marriage party up in the sanctuary, facing the people,
> and then stand facing them for the marriage ceremony.
> What is to be said of this?

The intention is admirable—to underline the fact that the
priest and worshipping community are witnesses to the
sacrament celebrated by the couple, the true ministers of
holy marriage. But the way it is carried out is deplorable
and clumsy. Out of human considerations it may even be
pastorally insensitive. It makes the couple and their attendants into a kind of stage show—not exactly helpful for a
nervous bride and groom, let alone their attendants, who all
have to "face the audience", whether they like it or not. I
am told that this style of celebrating marriage is also favored
by our friends the photographers, not forgetting the little
man with the video camera and the lights . . .

It seems better to maintain the traditional arrangement
of the wedding party facing the altar and the celebrant facing the congregation. However, to emphasize the mutual
consent, through which the spouses enter the sacramental
covenant, the couple should turn and face each other while
they make their "marriage vows". The celebrant may hand
each of them the book or a card with the text so that they
can read the form of consent.

11.7 The Penitential Rite at Nuptial Mass

> Can the penitential rite be left out of a Nuptial Mass?

Yes. The revised marriage rite of 1990, *Ordo Celebrandi Mat-
rimonium*, provides for two ways of carrying out the entrance

procession at Nuptial Mass, followed by the sign of the cross
and the greeting (no. 51). After the greeting there may be
a longer introduction to the celebration with alternatives
(nos. 52, 53). Here a rubric is included, "Omittitur actus
paenitentialis", meaning that the penitential rite should be
omitted in these circumstances. Vernacular versions of the
revised rite of 1990 are not yet available in all languages.

11.8 Blessing Holy Water

> What would you say of the old practice of adding un-
> blessed water to holy water, which was thereby blessed if
> the quantity of added water was less than that already in
> the container?

There was a general permission for this, perhaps because
the old rite of blessing water was quite long. Under modern circumstances I believe the practice of adding unblessed
water to holy water is redundant, for two reasons. (1) Holy
water is to be blessed as a public liturgical act at the beginning of the celebration of Mass, within the rite of sprinkling ("Asperges"). This underlines the baptismal and mystical significance of the blessed water. This rite of blessing
and sprinkling may replace the penitential rite at any Sunday Mass including the Saturday night Mass, thus ensuring an ample supply of holy water at any time of the year.
(2) If a priest urgently needs to bless water outside Mass, he
can use the prayer provided in the rite at the beginning of
Mass. It is not a long prayer. I regret to note, however, that
the current ICEL translations of the second option for this
prayer, as well as the prayer for blessing salt, eliminate the
explicit references to Satan (*the enemy*) found in the Latin
original. The priest is not obliged to bless salt and add it

to the water, although I believe this laudable custom should be retained in the public rite.

11.9 *The Holy Oils*

Would the same line of argument follow for the Holy Oils?

Here we also face changed conditions and better practices that, I believe, make the adding of unblessed oil to the Holy Oils redundant. That practice was permitted in the former *Rituale* and was necessary in an era of persecution, for example, in Ireland and Britain during the penal times.

In responding to this question, it seems best to consider the case of each of the Holy Oils separately.

1. The Oil most frequently used in a pastoral situation is the Oil of the Sick. If the priest runs out of a supply or cannot have access to blessed Oil in a specific situation, he can bless the oil himself using a prayer provided when he celebrates the rite (cf. Canon 999). Moreover, in an emergency, he could use any vegetable oil, as may be inferred from Canon 847 §1.

2. The Oil of Catechumens is used in the pre-baptismal rites in the RCIA or during infant Baptism, and normally it is blessed by a bishop during the Mass of the Chrism. However, lacking this Oil during the RCIA process, a priest could bless it using the prayer of blessing provided in *The Roman Ritual, Christian Initiation of Adults*, no. 131 (U.S. edition, no. 102).

3. The Sacred Chrism can only be consecrated by a bishop. For Confirmation, the bishop usually brings his own chrismatory, with an ample supply of Chrism. For the post-

baptismal anointing of infants, the priest need use only a small amount of Chrism. In the situation where a priest is authorized to confirm as part of the RCIA or reconciliation of separated Christians, he should take care to ensure beforehand that there is adequate Chrism, but obviously even a very small amount would suffice for a valid anointing.

The growing practice of reserving the Holy Oils in a noble repository in the church involves using larger vessels. In parishes with public repositories, the clergy would have access to a more abundant supply of the sacramental Oils and would be able to share with their neighbors in cases of need. It should also be noted that the use of "old" Oils, that is, from an earlier liturgical year, is licit "in a case of necessity" (Canon 847 §1). However, the priest who finds himself in this situation should obtain a supply of Holy Oils for the current year as soon as possible.

11.10 Cleaning Altar Linen

Do the old rules still apply about cleaning linen used at the altar?

Since no contrary instruction has ever been given, we may assume that the reverent purification of sacred linens should still be observed. However, there is an explicit instruction in the case set out in the *General Instruction of the Roman Missal*, no. 239: "If any of the precious blood spills, the area should be washed and the water poured into the sacrarium." From this we may infer that the purifiers and any other linen that may have had contact with the Precious Blood should first be rinsed, and the rinsings should be poured down the sacrarium. The linen should be hung out to dry, and then the sacristan or others may proceed with the normal washings (cf. *Ceremonies of the Modern Roman Rite*, appendix 6, no. 855). Because restrictions on handling vessels and the corporal are no longer in force, these purifications may be delegated by a priest to any responsible person.

11.11 Disposing of "Old Holy Water"

Is it true that one may add old holy water to a larger amount of unblessed water and then pour it down any sink, since it has lost its blessing?

By the expression "old holy water" I presume you refer to blessed water that has become unfit to use in a sacred action. This too can be poured down the sacrarium or onto clean earth when the vessel containing it is cleansed. The practice you describe seems permissible, but it does not seem to be worthy. Under modern circumstances we need to maintain worthy procedures.

12

EUCHARISTIC ADORATION

12.1 *Regulations for Exposition of the Blessed Sacrament*

> Years ago it was the custom wherever I was stationed
> for a letter from the bishop to be posted in every sac-
> risty declaring the times when eucharistic exposition and
> Benediction services were permitted. Is there any present
> legislation about this?

There is now no requirement that the Ordinary must indicate the only times when the Blessed Sacrament may be
exposed and when Benediction may be given. Pastors or
other priests with specific jurisdiction decide when public
eucharistic adoration takes place. It is now freely permitted "in all churches and oratories" (Canon 941 §1). But exposition may not take place during a Mass "celebrated in
the same area of the church or oratory" (Canon 941 §2).
Within his diocese the bishop can specify an obligatory time
of solemn annual adoration, envisaged in Canon 942, such as
the Forty Hours devotion, or he can require a time of public adoration for some specific intention. He can determine
whether there may be a public eucharistic procession, especially on Corpus Christi or some other appropriate occasion
(cf. Canon 944). The Canons emphasize that the liturgical
norms are to be observed at these celebrations.

12.2 Perpetual Adoration?

> In our diocese, a movement of lay people is promoting
> perpetual adoration of the Blessed Sacrament. But some
> liturgists are against it and have tried to persuade the
> bishop to forbid it, claiming it is against the modern lit-
> urgy. The lay group says that it is not breaking any litur-
> gical law. Who is right?

Here a distinction needs to be made between perpetual *adoration* and perpetual *exposition*. The diocesan liturgists may
have the impression that the latter is taking place in situations where no one is present to adore Our Lord, a practice
that is clearly forbidden. However, perpetual adoration before the tabernacle, based on a twenty-four-hour roster, is
within the law and would only cease during the celebration
of Mass or other rites in the same area where the Eucharist
is reserved. Some parishes have maintained this simple form
of rostered adoration, at least during the day, and the spiritual fruits, especially in terms of priestly and religious vocations, have been abundant. I was privileged to work in such
a parish for six years.

When we come to the second level, perpetual exposition
with a monstrance, some clarifications are needed. It is forbidden to expose the Blessed Sacrament while Mass or a
sacrament or funeral is being celebrated in the same area.
Therefore, a literally "perpetual" exposition would be im-
possible in the sanctuary of any church or chapel where the
liturgy is habitually celebrated. On the other hand, if the
Host is exposed in a separate chapel, which has been set
aside for this purpose, adoration may continue during rites
celebrated elsewhere in the church, because this is clearly

not the "same area". These provisions would also rule out giving Holy Communion to people from the sanctuary or in the chapel where the Blessed Sacrament is exposed. I have heard of such an unusual practice.

In the churches of religious congregations with a specific eucharistic identity, such as the Blessed Sacrament Fathers, exposition ceases while Mass is celebrated and recommences after Communion. During the Liturgy of the Hours, however, exposition continues because the Office may be sung or said before the Blessed Sacrament exposed. The example of these religious communities should guide parish adoration programs. But let no one argue, on the one hand, that perpetual adoration is "against the modern liturgy" or, on the other hand, that such adoration must be "perpetual" in a scrupulously literal sense.

When one hears of this dispute, it seems as if a few liturgists want to restrict eucharistic adoration as much as possible. They exaggerate "the rules" in a surprising way because they have their own agenda, but they are not in line with the mind of the Church. Therefore bishops and priests should carefully discern the motives behind legalistic opinions and theories that would even ban adoration, were this possible. Pastors should not let "experts" lead them into senseless conflict with devout members of Christ's faithful —who also can read official documents.

It is divisive and damaging when Catholics argue about the supreme devotion that is strongly encouraged by the Church, especially in an age when prayer should be encouraged as much as possible. Nevertheless, we should maintain a sense of balance, and exaggerations should be avoided. The essential laws must be observed prudently, in a spirit of toleration, and generous provision should be made for adoration. The Holy Spirit calls us to promote and not hinder this great outpouring of love, reparation and intercession within the Church.

12.3 Adoration Chapels

> In our parish a separate chapel has been built outside but near the church for eucharistic adoration, with perpetual exposition. Is this permitted?

There is no law against building such a chapel, provided the bishop permits it and the plans are in accord with liturgical law and custom. Separate eucharistic adoration chapels, apart from the church building or in a distinct area within the church that can be sealed off, are being set up in various places, for example, in the Philippines, where eucharistic devotion flourishes. These chapels have some advantages insofar as they can be used at times when the larger church has to be locked. On the other hand, they must be constantly maintained and supervised, preferably by a lay committee or sodality. The care of these chapels also raises a few problems that I wish to present in terms of concrete cases.

A friend of mine, who promotes eucharistic adoration in Australia, visited a parish where she found that a small wooden shed had been set up as the eucharistic chapel. She was shocked because the building and its appointments were scarcely worthy of the Holy Eucharist, and poverty was no excuse in this large busy parish! She was also shocked to find no one praying in the chapel. She made her holy hour alone, waiting for someone to turn up, but no one appeared. This lack of people present to adore Our Lord meant that anyone could have walked in and stolen the lunette containing the Sacred Host.

What then should have been done? In the case of this open chapel, the Eucharist should have been reposed until the time when people came to adore Our Lord. This can be easily arranged if laity or religious are authorized to repose and expose, or if the monstrance itself is contained in a kind of tabernacle that can easily be closed and locked. But let us suppose, for the sake of argument, that this chapel was securely locked, while exposition continued with no one present. I would argue that even in a locked chapel, to which people on a roster have access because they have received electronic keys, the practice of perpetual exposition is still illicit when no one is present, at least for *considerable* phases of time.

Some years ago, while in the Philippines, I visited one of these chapels, a handsome building built beside a large church. I was moved by the people's devotion in that holy place, but the chapel had been planned with complete disregard for the liturgy. The large monstrance was set into the wall, with a spotlight on it and various indoor plants were arranged in front of it. However no lamp was burning before the Sacrament, and not even the minimum four candles (or lamps) that are required during exposition were evident. Those details could easily have been attended to in this parish, where the chapel was visited by the faithful twenty-four hours a day, that is, day and night, with a guardian always present to maintain due order.

However, I was also surprised to find that there was no altar in this chapel. On this matter I believe we should follow the wise counsel of Pope Pius XII that the reserved Sacrament should never be separated from an altar. Today, when Mass is usually celebrated "facing the people", this does not mean that the tabernacle has to be set directly on an altar, rather that the focus of adoration should at least be visually *near* an altar. Celebration and adoration are thus linked; our eucharistic adoration flows from the celebration of the Eucharist and leads us back into the riches of the Church's liturgy. Therefore Mass should be celebrated from time to time on the altar of every adoration chapel, and eucharistic Benediction should be given there, during celebrations of communal adoration. These chapels are not set up merely for a "private devotion", like the shrine of a saint. Unfortunately these organic links with the liturgy were not evident in this unusual eucharistic chapel I visited in a land renowned for its fervor and devotion to our Eucharistic Lord.

12.4 Number Present at Benediction

> I am chaplain at a convent of missionary sisters who have exposition of the Blessed Sacrament, in a monstrance, every day, with Vespers, rosary and a final Benediction. Sometimes there are only two sisters present. Am I justified in carrying out exposition and Benediction in these circumstances?

There are no universal regulations now regarding the exact number of people who must be present at eucharistic exposition, so even when two sisters are present it would seem reasonable to proceed with exposition and to give the eucharistic blessing, Benediction, which forms part of the community life of this Congregation.

It is good to note that the sisters are aware that they can celebrate the Liturgy of the Hours (Divine Office) before the Blessed Sacrament exposed. For some years a legend has been circulating that this practice went "out" after the Council, but the *Ceremonial of Bishops*, no. 1111, certainly allows it, and the Liturgy of the Hours is linked to eucharistic adoration in the *Catechism of the Catholic Church*, no. 1178.

12.5 The Minister of Exposition

Who can expose and repose the Blessed Sacrament?

Those ordained to serve the Eucharistic Mystery, bishops, priests and deacons, can expose and repose the Blessed Sacrament. Since the Council, this duty has been extended to acolytes and other extraordinary ministers of the Eucharist, who have been *specifically authorized* for it by the Ordinary. Religious or lay people who are not extraordinary ministers but who are involved in regular eucharistic adoration may also seek this permission from the Ordinary. For the sake of lay ministers, I add a description of how exposition and reposition are to be carried out.

1. *Eucharistic Exposition:* The minister who exposes the Eucharist goes to the altar and unfolds the corporal, unless it has already been spread. (If a throne or tabor stand is used, a smaller corporal should already have been spread on it.) Then he comes before the tabernacle, unlocks it, genuflects and takes the pyx (containing the lunette) out of the tabernacle. The minister locks the tabernacle, sets the key to one side and then brings the pyx to the altar and places it on the corporal. The minister moves the monstrance to the left side of the corporal, turns it around and opens the glass panel. Then the minister opens the pyx, takes out the

lunette, places the Host reverently but securely in the monstrance and closes the glass panel. The monstrance is then reverently and precisely placed on the center of the corporal (or on the throne or tabor stand). The minister genuflects, and customary devotions or prayers may begin.

At the beginning of exposition, a priest or deacon may offer incense, and a hymn of adoration may be sung (cf. *Eucharistic Worship outside Mass*, nos. 88, 91, 92). A priest or deacon wears a white stole over an alb or cassock and surplice and may wear a cope. An acolyte wears an alb; a religious wears his or her habit; a lay person dresses modestly.

2. *Eucharistic Reposition:* The minister who reposes the Eucharist comes to the altar, genuflects, removes the lunette from the monstrance and puts it back into the pyx, which is immediately closed or covered. The minister places the monstrance to the left of the corporal and may veil it, if this is the local custom. Then the minister takes the pyx to the tabernacle, opens it, places the pyx in the tabernacle and genuflects *before* locking the door.

I would add that when no authorized person is present to repose the Eucharist when exposition is due to end, anyone present could repose the Eucharist. This unforeseen event should then be drawn to the attention of the pastor so that more people might be authorized to attend to this duty.

12.6 *Interrupting Exposition of the Blessed Sacrament*

A community of religious wants to have a day of exposition of the Blessed Sacrament, once a week, starting in the morning and ending before their evening meal. They take turns in adoring, but it is a small community. They want to know if exposition can be interrupted for their noon meal. If so, what is the procedure?

Yes, when there is not a sufficient number of worshippers, exposition may be interrupted, "But this may not be done more than twice a day, for example at midday and night" (*Eucharistic Worship outside Mass*, no. 88). Therefore, before the noon meal, the Blessed Sacrament could be reposed in the tabernacle by a priest, deacon, instituted acolyte or authorized extraordinary minister. Moreover, as noted above, the Ordinary could authorize the superior of the community or another brother or sister to repose the Eucharist (cf. *Eucharistic Worship outside Mass*, no. 91). After the noon meal, any of these persons could expose the Blessed Sacrament once more.

The simple rite of reposition is described in the reply to the preceding question. Candles and lamps on or around the altar of exposition should be extinguished for the time when exposition has ceased, leaving only the tabernacle lamp(s) burning. When exposition commences once more, the candles are lit, and the rite proceeds as described above. A hymn may be sung, and a priest or deacon presiding may offer incense.

There is no obligation to have Benediction at the conclusion of either the morning or evening period of adoration. Only a priest or deacon can give the eucharistic blessing. However, the ideal procedure for such a day of adoration would be as follows. The celebrant would expose the Blessed Sacrament immediately after Communion at the morning community Mass, using a Host consecrated at that Mass. The Mass would end with the Prayer after Communion. Exposition would cease during the noon meal, as described above. At the end of afternoon adoration, a priest or deacon would preside at Vespers and give Benediction. However, if a priest or deacon were not available for Vespers, the superior or another authorized brother or sister would repose the Eucharist after the Office, preferably while the community knelt and sang an appropriate hymn.

Adoration in religious communities, beginning with those dedicated to perpetual adoration, is strongly encouraged in *Eucharistic Worship outside Mass*, no. 90. Yet the perverse myth still persists that such practices are "out" now. Those who study *Eucharistic Worship outside Mass* find that the true mind of the postconciliar Church is *strongly* in favor of adoration of our Eucharistic Lord.

12.7 *Preaching during Exposition of the Blessed Sacrament*

In the past, the priest was forbidden to preach during exposition of the Blessed Sacrament, unless it was a brief talk on the Eucharist. A small banner ("bannerette") was placed in front of the monstrance during such a short sermon. Does all this still apply?

Preaching in the presence of the Blessed Sacrament exposed is mentioned explicitly in the current rite: "To encourage a prayerful spirit, there should be readings from scripture with a homily or brief exhortations to develop a better understanding of the eucharistic mystery" (*Eucharistic Worship outside Mass*, no. 95). Therefore homilies and "talks" are allowed, but the emphasis on a *brief* discourse remains in force. Too much preaching during adoration is discouraged. It is interesting to note, in the context of the spread of adoration in parishes, that our people are rediscovering the inestimable value of silence before the Lord.

Obviously the theme of preaching in this situation should be related to Our Lord in the Eucharist. In his comportment, words and gestures the preacher should show a devout awareness of the Presence of our Eucharistic Lord. Reverence would also suggest that the preacher should observe the custom of never turning his back on the monstrance. Naturally, he would make the appropriate reverence whenever passing in front of the altar of exposition. But there is no need to place anything in front of the monstrance during this kind of homily or sermon. In my opinion, such a practice would even detract from the intended effect of the words of the preacher.

12.8 *The Rosary during Exposition*

Is it permissible to say the rosary during eucharistic exposition?

The rosary is not primarily a Marian devotion. It is a Christ-centered method of meditation in a Marian form. It takes us through the saving Mysteries, the Incarnation, the Passion and Resurrection of Jesus Christ, with and through His Mother Mary. In the Eucharist, we celebrate and are united to these Mysteries of joy, sorrow and glory. They are made present in the Lord's Sacrifice. Therefore, the rosary in itself *can* be related to the Eucharist.

Therefore I am sure no pastor would presume to forbid anyone from silently saying the rosary in union with Mary before her Son, that is, during adoration of our Eucharistic Lord. But I can understand why some authorities have asked adoration groups not to recite the rosary *aloud* during exposition. Silence is the best "language" of adoration, and the rosary said aloud may seem distracting.

However, I believe the practice should be allowed, or at least tolerated, out of pastoral respect for the Catholics who give up their time, especially at all-night vigils, to adore the Lord Jesus and to make reparation. But I would suggest some conditions to help make a recited rosary more acceptable in this context. (a) Let it be recited reverently, without haste, in a reflective way and not too loudly. (b) Let the leader(s) relate the Mysteries to the Holy Eucharist, by some reflection before each decade or by relevant verses of Scripture. This can open up a whole new perspective of what the Eucharist is and how the liturgy brings the saving work of the Lord to us here and now. (c) Let it only be said when all present are prepared to join in, that is, when they know it is on the program. (d) Except for meditative reflections and scriptural verses, let it be free of "trimmings".

In these questions of licit personal devotions and popular forms of prayer, a generous and tolerant spirit should guide us all.

12.9 *The Exposition Throne?*

Can the permanent throne, which is behind the altar in some churches, still be used for exposition?

Yes—but only provided it is not "too distant" (cf. *Eucharistic Worship outside Mass, Rite of Eucharistic Exposition and Benediction*, no. 93). Here we find the renewed rules for exposition reflecting the principle laid down by Pope Pius XII, to which I have already referred: the place of celebration should not be separated from the place of reservation or adoration. Therefore, during exposition and Benediction it seems preferable to place the monstrance on a corporal spread on the altar.

But on the altar, a portable throne or a "tabor stand" may be used to add dignity or solemnity to eucharistic exposition or to help make the Host more easily visible in a large church.

12.10 *Illuminating the Exposition Throne*

> I believe it was forbidden to have an electric light illuminating the exposition throne. Does this rule still hold?

No. This minor rule simply fell into disuse. It was probably enacted to eliminate a vulgar tendency to adorn altars with electric lights, dating from the era when electricity was still a novelty and when electric globes created a dazzling effect that was regarded as "theatrical". But in practice it has become customary in many places to illuminate the throne or tabor stand, where this is used for exposition of the Blessed Sacrament. If done with taste, using modern lighting technology, this illumination can help focus our attention on the Sacred Host. I have even seen a laser beam used effectively to draw attention to the Host, exposed in a simple monstrance that was placed directly on an altar. It is also increasingly common to find the tabernacle illuminated with a concealed form of lighting. If this is not exaggerated, it can be helpful in drawing attention to the Real Presence, especially in a dark church. Nevertheless this kind of illumination could never be a substitute for the lamp that is to burn always near the tabernacle, even when permission has been granted to use an electric globe in that eucharistic lamp.

12.11 *The Corporal for Exposition*

> I was told that the same corporal should not be used for
> Mass and for eucharistic exposition and Benediction. Is
> this correct?

In the past, when the bread was consecrated resting on the
linen corporal, this may have been the practice in some
places. However, I cannot find this rule in such notable preconciliar authorities as Fortescue, O'Connell or O'Kane. If
the practice was observed in order to avoid small fragments
of the Host clinging to the base of the monstrance, then the
same objection could have been made to placing the chalice
and ciboria on the corporal, or to placing the monstrance on
the corporal at the end of the Mass on Corpus Christi Day,
just before the eucharistic procession. Today we need not
be concerned because the Eucharist is consecrated on the
paten, and fragments are less likely to be found on the corporal. Nevertheless the set of Benediction vestments usually
includes a burse in which is kept a corporal to be placed on
the altar, or throne or tabor stand, but this is out of convenience and not to avoid any supposed danger of irreverence.

12.12 *Candles and Lamps during Exposition*

> What is the minimum number of candles to be used at
> exposition? I have seen two used. I have also seen flicker-
> ing electric bulbs used instead of candles. If candles are
> used, must they be 50 percent beeswax?

At least four candles are required during exposition of the
Blessed Sacrament with a monstrance. Strictly speaking, six
candles is the maximum number proposed (cf. *Eucharistic*

Worship outside Mass, no. 85), no doubt to make the candles used at exposition parallel to those used during the celebration of Mass. In practice, however, we should recognize and welcome a laudable tendency to be flexible here and to increase the number of candles beyond the statutory six, at least during the major celebrations of solemn exposition and eucharistic Benediction. Extra candlesticks or candelabra may still be placed on the altar of exposition, or they may be arranged near it. However, two candles suffice when the ciborium is taken from the tabernacle for a simple form of adoration.

These lights should be real candles or lamps fed by wax or oil. The latter may be found to be more convenient during longer periods of exposition, for example in a perpetual adoration chapel. Using electric lights in place of candles during exposition is cheap and vulgar, hence unworthy. While the bishop may permit an electric sanctuary lamp in some situations, this concession does not extend to the candles used during the liturgy, and formal eucharistic adoration is to be understood as an extension of the liturgy, not a "devotion" added to the liturgy.

The old regulation concerning the 50 percent or 25 percent beeswax content no longer seems to be binding. In some countries this was never easy to observe and hence was modified. However, it is important to retain a sense of worthiness and always to ensure that good quality candles are set aside for this sacred purpose, in accord with the best that the local culture would want to offer to God. This is a question not only of aesthetics but of maintaining the continuity of our tradition where the lights fed by wax or oil have always been signs that indicate an offering of ourselves to God, our reverent homage and our human way of marking a solemn and sacred period of time.

13

CEREMONIES DURING
THE CHURCH YEAR

13.1 Holy Thursday: Washing of the Feet

Should the priest wash women's feet at the Washing of
Feet on Holy Thursday night?

The washing of the feet of twelve "men" is specified in the
Roman Missal, clearly to represent the twelve apostles. That
is the classical tradition, required by the Latin word *viri* for
those whose feet will be washed (cf. *Roman Missal, Evening
Mass of the Lord's Supper, Washing of Feet*, and *Ceremonial of
Bishops*, no. 301). The Holy See would have to grant a permission for a change in this tradition.

Some may claim that the authorization of female altar
servers makes it more difficult not to include women among
those whose feet will be washed. In this case, it is argued that
the symbolism now extends to include all believers and not
only the apostles. However, if ever a permission is granted in
favor of this view, one would hope that the group of twelve
persons would include both sexes. Washing *only* the feet of
women, as has happened in some places, is an ideological
statement, and the sacred liturgy must never be subjected
to ideology. This is why the Plenary Meeting of the Congregation for Divine Worship, May 1987, reacted strongly
against the proposal as something coming from feminism
(cf. *Notitiae*, no. 255 [October 1987], pp. 1017–18).

13.2 *Washing Hands instead of Feet?*

What is to be said of washing hands instead of feet on Holy Thursday night?

Not much at all. I cannot see the point of this practice. It can only satisfy the fastidious, who are not comfortable with Jesus, the Suffering Servant, kneeling to wash the feet of fishermen. In John 13:9 we read that one of them, St. Peter, objected, but once he saw what Our Lord was about, he wanted his hands and head washed as well; yet Our Lord insisted only on the humblest sign of washing feet. Hence, any substitute for this action only erases the radical sign of self-abasement and union with the Suffering Servant and His Covenant.

One may also ask what washing hands might mean in the context of the celebration of Our Lord's Paschal Mystery? The only hand-washing recorded in the Passion accounts was the deplorable self-absolution of Pontius Pilate. I am sure no one would want that gesture to insinuate itself into the Sacred Triduum.

13.3 *Good Friday: Veneration of the Cross*

Because it takes so long to venerate the cross on Good Friday, in one parish they pass a small crucifix around the church for everyone to kiss.

This is liturgical minimalism—a reduced sign carried out in the easiest way. The goal here is probably to save time. But a pastor should make it clear to his people that the Good Friday ceremonies will take time, because the Passion and death of our Savior took time. This is why the Church recommends the afternoon celebration commencing at 3 P.M. We offer our time out of gratitude and love for the One who entered time and died and rose for us in our flesh.

Another dimension of this example of liturgical minimalism is the way it turns what is both a corporate and personal act of veneration into only an act of private devotion. This is scarcely in line with the public worship of the Church and the renewal envisaged by the Fathers of the Second Vatican Council.

13.4 Rearranging the Easter Vigil

A priest I know has rearranged the Easter Vigil in his parish. He has the Scripture readings first, in a darkened church, and then he brings the Easter candle into the church for a ceremony of light. What is to be said of this adaptation?

What you describe is a well-intentioned, but mistaken, attempt to make the series of Old Testament readings "lead up to" the Resurrection, symbolized by bringing the candle into the church and by the sung Exsultet. This is didactic, and at first sight it seems logical, but it lacks the depth, richness and subtlety of the classical rite. It also sacrifices the involvement of the people in the procession into the darkened church, led by the light of the Easter candle, the symbol of the risen Lord. The people become observers rather than participants. But my criticism is best made by looking at the positive value of what the Church offers us in the official Vigil rite.

The structure of this ancient rite, carefully retained through two modern reforms (1955 and 1969), is based on a different symbolism. We first gather outside in the darkness around the new fire of Easter. The fire is blessed, the candle is lit, and "Christ our light" leads us out of darkness into His Church, a sign of our passover journey. His light spreads to us as we kindle our hand candles from the Easter candle. In the church, lit by the Easter candle and our candles, we celebrate the risen Lord in the sung Exsultet. We then hear the word of God proclaimed in His light, because only in that light of Resurrection can we comprehend the unfolding revelation of the prophecies that point to the Paschal Mystery. The light expands with the sung Gloria as the altar candles are lit and the bells sound joyously. Now we are ready for the celebration of the sacraments of Christian initiation, the renewal of the baptismal promises and the festive Eucharist. The liturgy thus expresses not only glory but that subtle hiddenness of the Resurrection that runs through the four Gospels. The Resurrection is only revealed to those who can comprehend it, to those who have been prepared and enlightened by the risen Lord Himself.

Any kind of unauthorized experimentation with the Easter Vigil is only "rearranging the furniture". The real challenge the Vigil puts before us is to deepen the quality of the celebration as we have it in the missal. This can be achieved through better music and hymns, good ceremonial carried out by well-trained servers, choosing lectors who can put expression into the readings, providing a variety of music for the psalms and canticles between the readings, giving a good Resurrection homily and cultivating a sense of splendor and festive joy through the visible signs of noble vessels, vestments, lights, incense and flowers. It is all "there". It is up to us to bring forth things old and new from the treasury of the Easter liturgy.

14

FUNERALS

14.1 Placing Symbols on the Coffin

At funerals, all sorts of things are now put on the coffin to symbolize the dead person's life. I even saw a teapot placed on a nun's coffin! Is this permitted?

If we study the *Order of Christian Funerals* (Latin original, no. 38; U.S. funeral rites nos. 133, 134, 163) we see that there is provision for placing *Christian* symbols on the coffin. This would surely have added meaning if the Bible, missal or crucifix so used really belonged to the deceased. But I do not think that a teapot qualifies as a Christian symbol. At the same time, we must impute sincerity to those who put the teapot on the coffin, no doubt with words explaining the homely details of sister's life of service. But the place for referring to her warmth and Christian hospitality would be in the homily—and here I would *slightly* bend the rule that forbids any trace of a panegyric or eulogy during the homily. It should be noted in the U.S. rite that the symbol is placed on the casket in silence or using a prescribed text (cf. U.S. rites, no. 400).

As I have already remarked, sentimentality is a perennial inspiration for liturgical nonsense. Therefore the liturgy descends to the depths of banality when the bric-a-brac of Aunt Maud are arranged on her casket. Sentimental acts can also misfire and become pastorally insensitive, for example, placing a favorite toy on the casket of a small child could be a very cruel gesture to some members of the immediate family.

14.2 Funeral Readings: Poems and Popular Music?

> At the funeral of a friend of mine, we were told that the Scripture readings had been chosen because these were his favorite texts. One of his favorite poems was read during the service. I also heard a favorite pop song sung at the funeral of a young man. Is this kind of adaptation permitted?

A wide range of Scripture readings is set out in the lectionary and the *Order of Christian Funerals*, and only these are to be used at Catholic funerals. The family or friends of the deceased should be invited to choose from these readings, in consultation with the celebrant. Once you depart from what is offered in the rite, readings with little bearing on the liturgical action will inevitably appear. This may also lead to unintended absurdities.

A favorite poem might be incorporated or cited in the homily, if this is appropriate, but it must never replace a psalm or reading. A favorite *religious* poem, with orthodox content, could be used after Communion if it seemed appropriate as a reflection or thanksgiving. At the graveside, a member of the family or a friend may wish to read a favorite poem, but let this be done before or after the prayers for Christian burial so that it is not part of the Rite of Committal.

Singing favorite songs at funerals only seems to raise more problems. Even some religious items are well outside our

Catholic tradition and may include false doctrine, not to mention a vulgar style. These songs may never replace the responsorial psalm or the antiphons or hymns. Because sentimentality may be insinuating itself once more, singing a favorite pop song or ethnic ballad, especially during the final procession, may even intensify the grief of those who mourn. If family or friends insist on including this kind of music, let it be done at the graveside; but like the poetry, it should not be part of the Catholic Rite of Committal.

Unintended absurdity can also arise when popular music is included in a funeral. I knew a beloved pastor who was accustomed to play musical cassettes when there was no organist available. Just before the final procession at a funeral, he hastily seized a cassette and put it into the public address system. The congregation watched the remains of the dear departed leave the church to the strains of Vera Lynn singing "We'll meet again. Don't know where. Don't know when."

These incongruities underline the need for the celebrant of the funeral rites to control the situation and to *know beforehand exactly what will happen*. He may have to bend on small matters, but he should strive to maintain the integrity and dignity of the Christian rites. The same applies to the use of poetry and popular music at the celebration of marriage, although it is easier to control bad taste in this less emotionally charged situation. The Ordinary may wish to legislate on these matters, not only to uphold the sacred liturgy but to protect his priests from unfair criticism when they make a stand for good taste and noble worship.

14.3 Homily or Eulogy?

> I have been to funerals where the homily was simply a
> eulogy devoted to the life of the deceased. I thought this
> was forbidden.

Yes, it is forbidden (cf. *Order of Christian Funerals*, no. 141).
The brief homily is not meant to be a eulogy or a panegyric
in honor of the deceased. Many of us have been to funerals where this kind of discourse has not merely descended
to sentimentality or triviality but risen to the heights of a
solemn proclamation of beatification, if not an instant can-
onization! On the other hand, it would be difficult, if not
callous, to exclude any reference to the deceased from the
homily. This is why I think that pastoral common sense
would modify a total ban of any comment on the life or
character of the Christian soul we are commending to the
merciful Lord. But most of the content and the main emphasis of the homily should consist of drawing out the revealed truths from the chosen readings, that is, proclaim-
ing the consoling, but challenging, facts of life and death,
resurrection, judgment, purgatory and our hope of eternal
life in heaven. This is a great opportunity for evangelizing
because non-Christians apparently find the Catholic rites
to be the most interesting and consoling of any funerals
they attend. Here is one of those moments in the modern
world when people are forced to face reality. Without being
heavy-handed, we should seize such moments and use them
for the glory of the risen Lord and the salvation of souls.

In some places a eulogy is given after the Prayer after
Communion and before the Rite of Final Commendation
and Farewell. This is allowed according to the *Order of Christian Funerals*, U.S. rite, no. 197: "A member or a friend of

the family may speak in remembrance of the deceased." Note that one person may speak, not seven people—who spoke for well over three quarters of an hour (the last man took twelve minutes) at the funeral of a popular young person! This may seem to be the right time for such words, as long as they are brief, but it is not appropriate to intrude a eulogy into the Rite of Final Commendation and Farewell celebrated at the casket. However, when all things are considered, I believe it is preferable to postpone any kind of eulogy to the rite of Christian burial, just before the prayers of committal.

14.4 *The Color of Funeral Vestments*

> Recently, I was surprised to see a young priest wearing black eucharistic vestments and even a black cope at a funeral. I thought that went out years ago!

The *option* of wearing black vestments has never "gone out". Black *may* be used: (a) for All Souls Day, (b) for funerals, and (c) for Masses for the dead ("Requiems") (cf. *General Instruction of the Roman Missal*, no. 308 e). In Western countries or in other communities where black is still regarded as a respectful traditional color for these celebrations, any priest should be free to choose black, and a noble set of these vestments should be available in the sacristy.

I note that the priest was "young", an interesting detail for anyone who is really reading the "signs of the times" today. I note that he also wore a cope, presumably for the Final Commendation. He also knew that replacing the chasuble with a cope for that rite remains an option, whatever color one chooses to wear. But I am not going to defend his choice to wear black on this occasion, because I do not know the pastoral situation in which he celebrated these funeral rites.

Pastoral common sense and some liturgical considerations need to guide us through the furrows of this widely discussed, and far from trivial, question. For thirty years, purple has been widely used in some countries, such as Italy, where liturgists have tried to wean the people away from the lugubrious funeral customs of the past. On the other hand, white has also become virtually universal in the United States, Canada, Australia and New Zealand, where liturgists want to emphasize the hope of the Resurrection. White is also required in some Asian countries, where it is the cultural color of *mourning*. Therefore, choosing black in any of these situations would need to be based on some serious reasons, not forgetting pastoral sensitivity to the wishes of the family of the deceased. I hope that young priest acted with pastoral responsibility.

It must be admitted, however, that *always* wearing white and concentrating on the joy of eternal life has caused problems at some funerals. This approach can take away the right and the *need* to mourn, which is essential in certain situations. A widow once published an article in the U.S. Catholic Press expressing her anger at the joyous celebration of her husband's resurrection, which took no account of her grief. Some funerals in white vestments have also become those "instant canonizations", even in cases where neither the deceased nor those present would have wanted such pretense. Here, purple could help create a more honest and serious mood, focused on penitence and purgatory.

One interesting resolution to this problem has been to design a specific set of white funeral vestments (with a matching pall to cover the casket). These vestments are of a much simpler design than the noble white or gold vestments used for other celebrations. Moreover, they may appropriately incorporate some of the more traditional funeral colors: black, dark gray and purple. They could be adorned with symbols that evoke the Resurrection and eternal life.

I personally hold that black should be worn at least once a year, on All Souls Day, when a serious reflection on our mortality can be appropriately combined with prayer for the dead. But in all these matters, let priests respect the freedom of other priests. Let us never seek to forbid our brethren to use what the Church still allows them—even if it is now only an option that we may not favor.

APPENDIX

THE OXFORD DECLARATION

The Centre for Faith and Culture based at Westminster College, Oxford, held a conference in June 1996 on the future of the liturgy under the challenging theme, "Beyond the Prosaic". At the conclusion of the conference, the participants, constituted as the Liturgy Forum, agreed upon the following declaration.

1. Reflecting on the history of liturgical renewal and reform since the Second Vatican Council, the Liturgy Forum agreed that there have been many positive results. Among these might be mentioned the introduction of the vernacular, the opening up of the treasury of the Sacred Scriptures, increased participation in the liturgy and the enrichment of the process of Christian initiation. However, the Forum concluded that the preconciliar liturgical movement as well as the manifest intentions of *Sacrosanctum Concilium* have in large part been frustrated by powerful contrary forces, which could be described as bureaucratic, philistine and secularist.

2. The effect has been to deprive the Catholic people of much of their liturgical heritage. Certainly, many ancient traditions of sacred music, art and architecture have been all but destroyed. *Sacrosanctum Concilium* gave pride of place to Gregorian chant, yet in many places this sung theology of the Roman liturgy has disappeared without trace. Our litur-

gical heritage is not a superficial embellishment of worship but should properly be regarded as intrinsic to it, as it is also to the process of transmitting the Catholic faith in education and evangelization. Liturgy cannot be separated from culture; it is the living font of a Christian civilization and hence has profound ecumenical significance.

3. The impoverishment of our liturgy after the Council is a fact not yet sufficiently admitted or understood, to which the necessary response must be a revival of the liturgical movement and the initiation of a new cycle of reflection and reform. The liturgical movement which we represent is concerned with the enrichment, correction and resacralization of Catholic liturgical practice. It is concerned with a renewal of liturgical eschatology, cosmology and aesthetics, and with a recovery of a sense of the sacred—mindful that the law of worship is the law of belief. This renewal will be aided by a closer and deeper acquaintance with the liturgical, theological and iconographic traditions of the Christian East.

4. The revived liturgical movement calls for the promotion of the Liturgy of the Hours, celebrated in song as an action of the Church in cathedrals, parishes, monasteries and families, and of Eucharistic Adoration, already spreading in many parishes. In this way, the Divine Word and the Presence of Christ's reality in the Mass may resonate throughout the day, making human culture into a dwelling of God. At the heart of the Church in the world we must be able to find that loving contemplation, that adoring silence, which is the essential complement to the spoken word of Revelation and the key to active participation in the holy mysteries of faith.

5. We call for a greater pluralism of Catholic rites and uses, so that all these elements of our tradition may flourish and be more widely known during the period of reflection and *ressourcement* that lies ahead. If the liturgical movement is to prosper, it must seek to rise above differences of opinion and taste to that unity which is the Holy Spirit's gift to the Body of Christ. Those who love the Catholic tradition in its fullness should strive to work together in charity, bearing each other's burdens in the light of the Holy Spirit and persevering in prayer with Mary the Mother of Jesus.

6. We hope that any future liturgical reform would not be imposed on the faithful but would proceed, with the utmost caution and sensitivity to the *sensus fidelium*, from a thorough understanding of the organic nature of the liturgical traditions of the Church. Our work should be sustained by prayer, education and study. This cannot be undertaken in haste, or in anything other than a serene spirit. No matter what difficulties lie ahead, the glory of the Paschal Mystery —Christ's love, his cosmic sacrifice and his childlike trust in the Father—shines through every Catholic liturgy for those who have eyes to see, and in this undeserved grace we await the return of spring.

June 29, 1996, Solemnity of St. Peter and St. Paul